ANTIGUA AND BARBUDA
A Little Bit of Paradise

SEVENTH EDITION

Edited by Arif Ali

HANSIB

First published in Great Britain by Hansib Publications in 2016

Hansib Publications Limited
P.O. Box 226, Hertford, SG14 3WY
United Kingdom

info@hansibpublications.com
www.hansibpublications.com

ISBN 978-1-910553-70-1 *Hardback*
ISBN 978-1-910553-71-8 *Paperback*

First edition published by Hansib Publications in 1988
Second edition published by Hansib Publications in 1994
Third edition published by Hansib Publications in 1996
Fourth edition published by Hansib Publications in 1999
Fifth edition published by Hansib Publications in 2005
Sixth edition published by Hansib Publications in 2008

A CIP catalogue record for this book
is available from the British Library

Design and production by Hansib Publications
United Kingdom

CONTENTS

Message from the Prime Minister 4

Message from the Minister of Tourism, Economic Development, Investment & Energy 5

Acknowledgements 6

Map of Antigua and Barbuda 7

Antigua and Barbuda Facts & Figures 8

National Anthem song sheet 10

National Heroes 11

Antigua and Barbuda at Thirty-Five 13

History Timeline 15

Introduction 16

Barbuda 55

A day out in Antigua and Barbuda 63

Antigua and Barbuda by bus 88

The parishes of Antigua and Barbuda 90

Education 113

The arts 117

A rich literary tradition 125

Carnival in Antigua and Barbuda 126

Antigua Sailing Week 141

Nelson's Dockyard 149

A hero's welcome for Team Wadadli 158

World-class marine administration 159

Natural wonders 160

A safe haven for donkeys 170

Sport in Antigua and Barbuda 172

Religion 185

Rastafari in Antigua and Barbuda 190

A paradise for food-lovers 192

Raising the spirits 196

Agriculture 198

Shopping in Paradise 209

Getting married in Antigua and Barbuda 216

Business growth and development in paradise 218

China relations blossom 220

Housing 224

The Defence Force at Thirty-Five 228

Taking the profit out of crime 229

Antigua and Barbuda is going green 231

Antigua and Barbuda is a medical nexus 232

The American University of Antigua College of Medicine 232

Advocacy in Antigua and Barbuda 233

Italian language synopsis 234

Chinese language synopsis 236

Arabic language synopsis 239

MESSAGE FROM THE PRIME MINISTER

I am delighted and honoured to be presenting to the whole world, for their pleasure and for posterity, the Seventh Edition of *A Little Bit of Paradise.* This important publication, supported by countless photos, presents an image of Antigua and Barbuda that is exquisitely the work of Hansib Publications.

As we celebrate the 35th Anniversary of Independence and the 60th Anniversary of Carnival, the ability to capture these important milestones as the nation matures is the task assigned to *A Little Bit of Paradise.*

The private sector in Antigua and Barbuda has made a significant contribution to this edition, and I thank these enterprises for their participation. The Government will continue to do its part to promote Antigua and Barbuda utilizing every tool available. *A Little Bit of Paradise* is a great promotional device for ensuring Antigua and Barbuda's success as a rich historical and beautiful destination, filled with wonderful people, is told to all the world.

I invite those who examine these pages, but who have not yet seen our country, to visit Antigua and Barbuda. Our country is one of the most-sought-after investment destinations in

the region, with guarantees of return that will make you love it even more. You are also guaranteed to experience all the joys so evident on the faces of those who have been captured by the camera on these pages. Enjoy!

Honourable Gaston Browne
Prime Minister

WELCOME TO A LITTLE BIT OF PARADISE

After an absence of several years "A Little Bit of Paradise" has returned better than ever as a refreshing publication that showcases and uncovers the breathtaking beauty of the country and people of the beautiful twin-island nation of Antigua and Barbuda. Our islands stand out as an undeniably safe, beautiful and exciting haven for locals and visitors alike. From the bliss of the trade winds to the remarkable beauty of our pristine 365 pink and white sandy beaches there is something enticing and pleasurable for everyone to enjoy.

As the Minister of Tourism, Economic Development Investment and Energy, it is with immense pleasure that I say to all, *"Come and enjoy a Little Bit of Paradise"* because the experience of being in Antigua and Barbuda promises to be an unforgettable one. The twin-isle paradise blossoms with delight, relaxation and fun for the entire family.

Next year will be a major anniversary year for Antigua and Barbuda, with a packed calendar of not to be missed events. We invite you to experience Antigua and Barbuda's Carnival, appropriately dubbed the Caribbean's greatest summer festival, as we celebrate its 60th anniversary. With Sailing Week celebrating its 50th Anniversary, and the Antigua Classic Yacht Regatta commemorating 30 years of world-class yachting we have cemented our position as the mecca of Caribbean sailing. These celebrations will all be held in the historic Nelson's Dockyard recently designated by UNESCO as a 'World Heritage Site'.

These are just a few of the amazing things that will leave you with a lifetime of unforgettable, wonderful memories when you visit us in Antigua and Barbuda. The rhythms, historical sites, unique attractions and culinary delights for which our guests from all over the world keep coming year after year will cause you to fall in love with our beautiful islands.

A Little Bit of Paradise brings to life the tropical essence and flavour of our islands while capturing the true spirit, strength and rich character of our people. A stay in Antigua and Barbuda will offer our visitors a unique experience with unforgettable positive memories that will last you a lifetime; it will, as we give you a true taste of the authentic Antigua and Barbuda.

This publication has differentiated itself by vividly describing and sharing the many spectacular features and attractions of our country that will match the taste and travelling budget of any visitor and so we are grateful to all those whose creativity and collaboration has made this delightful publication a reality.

For those seeking an experiential and unforgettable vacation experience, a second home or just seeking to find out more about two of the most beautiful islands in the world, we invite you to dive into this award-winning publication that has captured the true essence and charm of Antigua and Barbuda. It is with a sense of pride that we present to you a true representation of who we are with this enduring issue of *A Little Bit of Paradise*.

Hon. Asot A. Michael
Minister of Tourism, Economic Development, Investment & Energy

ACKNOWLEDGEMENTS

Much gratitude goes to the following for their support and contributions to the 7th edition of *Antigua and Barbuda: A Little Bit of Paradise*.

Prime Minister Gaston Browne and the Antigua and Barbuda Cabinet for commissioning this edition. The new format was suggested by Prime Minister.

Special thanks to the Hon. Asot A. Michael, Minister of Tourism, Economic Development and Energy and his staff at the Ministry.

The former Minister of Trade, Industry and Commerce, Hugh Marshall, whose advice throughout the project was invaluable, and I am grateful to Chief of Staff Ambassador Lionel (Max) Hurst for much assistance and support and the staff at Prime Minister's Office.

Thanks are due to our ubiquitous **Managing Editor, Kash Ali**, and our UK team – Ella Barnes, Ansel Wong, Alan Cross, Shareef Ali, Richard Painter, Samantha Dewey, Ken Walker, Lisa Regan, Sayrah Ali and our translators Intonations Limited; Vino Patel; the management and staff at Heritage Hotel in Antigua; Khalda Hassan, Zorena Yhap, Merle Miller, Eustace Hurst and Malaka Parker.

Thank you former Prime Minister Sir Lester Bryant Bird.

To our coordinating team / editors in Antigua and Barbuda, Moti Persaud, Brenda Lee Browne, Joanne Hillhouse and Ivor Ford.

Thank you Sasha Stuart-Young, Bobby Reis, Aziz Hadeed, Rohan Hector, Michael Benjamin, Trevor Powell (Cadafy) and Arwain Christian.

Minister the Hon. E.P. Chet Green, Permanent Secretary Paula Frederick-Hunte, Colin James and Henderson Fields for your time, advice, action and support.

To our contributing writers (in alphabetical order): Zahra I. Airall, Major Telbert Benjamin, Mickel Brann-Challenger, Brenda Lee Browne, Sally Davis, Ivor B. Ford, Ras Franki/Franklin Francis, Daryl George, Michelle George, Joanne C. Hillhouse, D. Gisele Isaac, Natalya Lawrence, Dr Hazra C. Medica, Kimolisa Mings, Dr K.K. Singh, Brian Stuart-Young.

To our contributing photographers (in alphabetical order): Joseph Jones, Joseph Martin

Thank you to the following businesses / organisations for their invaluable support in ordering advance copies of the book (in alphabetical order):

Antigua and Barbuda Airport Authority (ABAA)
Antigua Computer Technology (ACT)
Antigua and Barbuda Defence Force (ABDF)
American University of Antigua (AUA)
Antigua and Barbuda Department of Marine Services & Merchant Shipping
Financial Service Regulatory Commission (FSRC)
Falmouth Harbour Marina
Global Bank of Commerce (GBC)
Hadeed Motors
Leewind Paints Ltd
Office of National Drug and Money Laundering Policy (ONDCP)
Percival Enterprise Ltd
Quin Farara Wines & Spirits
Royal Police Force of Antigua and Barbuda
Siboney Resort
Shoul's Toys and Gifts
Super Power
Tradewinds Hotel
Umaco-Protective Sealers
West Indies Oil Company

And finally to Pamela Mary for caring so much.

Arif Ali
November 2016

Map Key

═══════	Main Road
═══════	Secondary Road
───────	Other Road
··········	Track
─ ─ ─ ─	Runway
✈	Airport
	Customs & Immigration
• Police Stn	Police Station
	Gas Station
Ⓑ	Bus Station
PO	Post Office
Sch	School
†	Church
Ⓗ	Hospital
🚦	Traffic Light
△▽	Trigonomical Station
★	Point of Interest
⸺	Jetty/Jetties
	Beaches

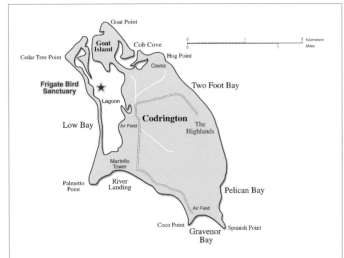

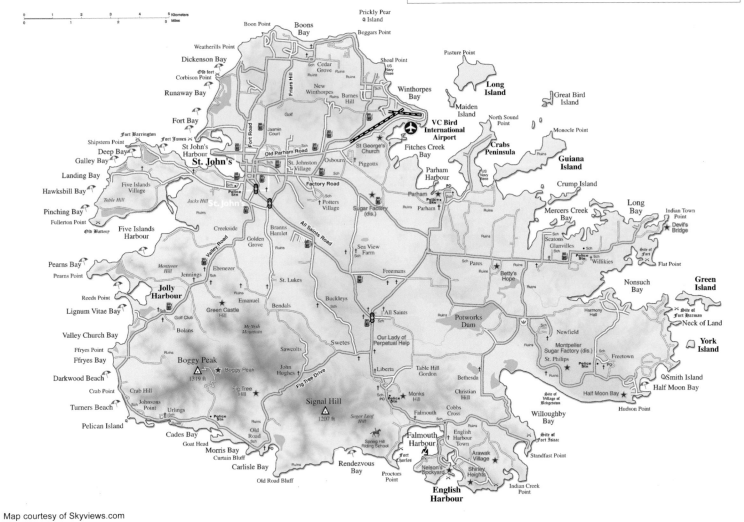

Map courtesy of Skyviews.com

7

Name: Antigua and Barbuda

Area: 442 sq km (170 sq miles) – Antigua 281 sq km; Barbuda 161 sq km

Location: The twin-island state of Antigua and Barbuda is situated in the Eastern Caribbean in the Leeward Islands chain. Antigua is the largest of the Leeward Islands and its sister island, Barbuda, is located approximately 30 miles north.

Population: 93,000 (2016 est.)

Capital: St John's (pop. 22,000 approx.)

Nationality: Antiguan, Barbudan

Language: English (official), Antiguan Creole

Religion / religious observance: Protestant (Anglican 18%, Seventh Day Adventist 12%, Pentecostal 12%, Moravian 8%, Methodist 6%, Wesleyan Holiness 4%, Church of God 4%, Baptist 3%); Roman Catholic 8%; other 12%; other 2%, none or unspecified 10%

Ethnic groups: African heritage 88%, mixed 5%, Hispanic 3%, white 2%, other 3%

Currency: East Caribbean Dollar and United States Dollar

Government: A constitutional, Westminster-style parliamentary democracy. The bicameral Legislature comprises a 17-member House of Representatives elected every five years (or earlier at the discretion of the sitting Prime Minister) and a Senate of 18 appointed members.

Main political parties: Antigua & Barbuda Labour Party (ABLP), Barbuda People's Movement (BPM) and the United Progressive Party (UPP) which is a coalition of three parties – Antigua Caribbean Liberation Movement (ACLM), Progressive Labour Movement (PLM) and the United National Democratic Party (UNDP)

Head of State: Queen Elizabeth II (since 1952) represented by Governor-General Sir Rodney E. Williams

Prime Minister: Gaston Browne (since 13 June 2014)

Administrative Divisions: Six parishes – St George, St John, St Mary, St Paul, St Peter and St Philip, and two dependencies – Barbuda and Redonda

Public Holidays: New Year's Day, Good Friday, Easter Monday, Labour Day (1 May), Whit Monday, Carnival (1st Monday in August), National Heroes' Day (26 October), Independence Day (1 November), V.C. Bird Day (9 December), Christmas Day, Boxing Day

Events: Antigua Yacht Club Round the Island Race (Jan), Black History Month (February), International Cricket (March), International Kite Festival (March), Antigua Open Golf Tournament (March), Antigua Classic Yacht Regatta (April), Antigua Sailing Week (April / May), Caribana in Barbuda (Whitsun weekend), Antigua and Barbuda Sports Fishing Tournament (May), Run in Paradise Half Marathon (May), Calypso Spectacular (June), Miss Antigua Pageant (June), Kitesurfing Camp at Nonsuch Bay (June), Classic Fishing Tournament and Sport Fishing Tournament (June), Carnival season (July / August), Wadadli Day (July), Mango Festival (July), Turtle-watching Season (July-September), Fishing Tournament and Seafood Festival

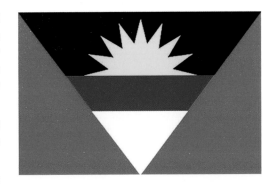

(September), Independence Ceremonial Parade and Food Fare (November), Best in the West Fishing Tournament (November), Jolly Harbour Yacht Club Annual Regatta (November), Antigua Charter Yacht Show (December)

Important dates: Independence from Great Britain, 1 November 1981. Joined the Commonwealth in 1981

International organisation participation: ACP, AOSIS, C, Caricom, CDB, CELAC, FAO, G-77, IBRD, ICAO, ICC (NGOs), ICCt, ICRM, IDA, IFAD, IFC, IFRCS, ILO, IMF, IMO, IMSO, Interpol, IOC, IOM, ISO (subscriber), ITU, ITUC (NGOs), MIGA, NAM (observer), OAS, OECS, OPANAL, OPCW, Petrocaribe, UN, UNCTAD, UNESCO, UPU, WFTU (NGOs), WHO, WIPO, WMO, WTO

Major industries: Tourism, construction, light manufacturing, financial services

The economy: Tourism continues to dominate Antigua and Barbuda's economy, accounting for nearly 60% of GDP and 40% of investment. The twin-island nation's agricultural production caters largely for the domestic market. Manufacturing comprises small assembly for export with major products being bedding, handicrafts and electronic components.

Agricultural products: Cotton, fruits, vegetables, bananas, coconuts, cucumbers, mangoes, sugarcane, livestock

Climate: Tropical with little variation between the seasons

Highest Point: Mount Obama (formerly Boggy Peak), 402 m/1319 ft

Internet Country Code: .ag

International Dialling Code: +1 268

National Flag: Red, with an inverted isosceles triangle based on the top edge of the flag; the triangle contains three horizontal bands of black (top), blue and white, with a yellow rising sun in the black band; the sun symbolises the dawn of a new era, black represents the African heritage of most of the population, blue is for hope, and red is for the dynamism of the people; the 'V' stands for victory; the successive yellow, blue and white colouring is also meant to evoke the country's tourist attractions of sun, sea and sand.

Coat of Arms: Designed in 1966 by Gordon Christopher and officially introduced on 16 February 1967. At the top of the Coat of Arms is the Antigua black pineapple. The plants around the shield are red hibiscus, sugarcane and yucca. Supporting the shield is a pair of fallow deer representing the wildlife. The design on the shield shows the sun rising from a blue and white sea. The sun symbolises a new beginning and the black background represents the African origins of most of the nation's citizens.

At the bottom of the shield sits a stylised sugar mill. At the bottom is a scroll upon which is written the national motto: "Each endeavouring, all achieving".

National Flower: Agave (dagger log or batta log, century plant)

National Bird: Magnificent frigate bird (man-o-war or weather bird)

National Animal: Fallow deer

National Sea Creature: Hawksbill turtle

National Fruit: Antigua black pineapple

National Dish: Pepperpot and fungee

National Motto: "Each endeavouring, all achieving"

SIR VERE CORNWALL BIRD SR.
(1909-1999)
1st Chief Minister, 1st Premier and 1st
Prime Minister of Antigua and Barbuda

PRINCE KLAAS (KING COURT
TACKEY, KWAKU TAKYI)
(c1694-1736)
Executed leader of a failed slave revolt
in 1736

DAME GEORGIANA 'NELLIE'
ROBINSON
(1880-1972)
Founder of the T.O.R. Memorial School
which was the first secondary school to
admit 'illegitimate' children

SIR GEORGE HERBERT WALTER
(1928-2008)
2nd Premier of Antigua and Barbuda
(1971-1976)

SIR ISAAC VIVIAN 'VIV' ALEXANDER
RICHARDS, OBE
(1952-)
One of the greatest cricketers of all time

SIR LESTER BRYANT BIRD
(1938-)
2nd Prime Minister of Antigua and
Barbuda (1994-2004)

"The young adult years."

ANTIGUA AND BARBUDA AT THIRTY-FIVE

As the longest serving parliamentarian in Antigua and Barbuda, Sir Robin Yearwood vividly remembers 1 November 1981 when, at the stroke of midnight, the Union Flag was lowered and the Antigua and Barbuda flag was raised, signalling that the twin-island nation was sovereign.

"My body shivered and I was so happy when I saw the Antigua and Barbuda flag going up. A new feeling came over me and, honestly, tears fell. I said to myself, 'This is now mine, and I have to put my all into it if it is to survive'," Sir Robin, the Member of Parliament for St Philip North, said.

Antigua and Barbuda's positive mark on the world has, arguably, been made by sportsmen, notably legendary cricketer and National Hero, Sir Vivian Richards, and creatives such as the musical group, Burning Flames and long-transplanted writer, Jamaica Kincaid. At 35, outward symbols of the country's Independence are represented in the anthem, the flag and other iconography, as well as in the way it has fared over the course of three-and-a-half decades – with a healthy, peaceful, secure and egalitarian society.

Colin Murdoch was an overseas university student following the proceedings by radio when the country achieved political independence. His father, Hilson Murdoch, was the event's master of ceremonies. Today, the younger Murdoch is Permanent Secretary in the Office of the Prime Minister. He opined that the hallmarks of Antigua and Barbuda's independence are the investments that have led to development and economic growth.

And this is what political independence has birthed: GDP per capita, according to the World Bank, averaging just under US $20,000 for the period 1990 to 2015, and a ranking of 58 out of 188 countries in the 2014 Human Development Index. All this is good in the context of self-sufficiency and development, but being ranked as an upper-income country disqualifies the twin-island nation from most Overseas Developmental Assistance programs.

So, a measure of political independence is how Antiguans and Barbudans continue to evolve to meet the demands of an ever-changing world and shifting priorities.

It's marked not by big houses, luxury vehicles and other trappings, but by the grandparents and parents who turned ploughshares into bank shares, and whose box money and income earned from back-bending, punishing labour has funded tuition at

13

The beach at Crabbe Hill,
St Mary / JJ

secondary and tertiary level for offspring who now sit among the politicians and professionals moving the country forward. In Antigua and Barbuda today, it is becoming the norm, and not the exception, that the huckster's child is the district doctor, and so on.

Additionally, Antigua and Barbuda's independence agenda is largely linked to its interdependence, viewed by people like Murdoch, the country's ambassador to the OECS, as a pooling, rather than a ceding, of power. The country has formed several alliances and deepened others over the years, notably, the twenty-member Caribbean Community (CARICOM), with its Single Market and plans for a Single Economy, and the nine-member Organisation of Eastern Caribbean States (OECS). It is the benefits of these arrangements – and in the case of the OECS, the single and stable Eastern Caribbean currency, a shared central bank, harmonised legislation and procurement policies, regional institutions and, latterly, free movement – that show the gains since parting ways with Britain as an underdeveloped and under-funded associated state.

"These regional arrangements protect us and help us to attract development from the international world," said Ambassador Murdoch.

Ingenuity and courage will keep the country on the right track in attracting investment initiatives that will lead to further development, such as the nascent introduction of the Citizenship by Investment Program (CIP). A shift in the education paradigm, from preparing employees to cultivating the characteristics of entrepreneurship, is also the pathway to the future.

For Sir Robin, sustainability lies in the youth and in unrelenting nationalism. "There are times when I feel like I felt on that day, especially when I see little children singing folk songs and the anthem. It brings me back to 1981, and I think each time I see something like that, 'There's the beginning of a new era', but I'd love to see the nation display that kind of love every day. If we love the country and live up to our duties, we will continue to make strides."

If Independence can be taken to mean ownership, and ownership to mean managing responsibility, the record will show that though the vagaries of life, natural and man-made, have at times pushed the country down, Antigua and Barbuda always returns to its feet.

Mickel Brann-Challenger

HISTORY TIMELINE

3100 BCE First inhabitants were hunter-gatherer Amerindians known as the Siboney

100 CE Arawak peoples arrive followed by Caribs

1493 Christopher Columbus lands on Antigua and names it after the Church of Santa Maria de la Antigua in Seville, Spain

1628 Britain annexes Barbuda

1632 Sir Thomas Warner, Governor of the Leeward Islands, arrives from St Kitts

1650 Betty's Hope sugarcane plantation established

1652 France claims Antigua

1666 First successful settlement on Barbuda

1667 France ends its claim to Antigua in accordance with the Treaty of Breda and Antigua becomes a British colony

1674 English sugar planter, Christopher Codrington sets up a plantation in Antigua

1685 Codrington leases Barbuda from the British crown; enslaved Africans brought to Antigua to work on the plantations

1736 Planned slave rebellion uncovered resulting in the execution of nearly one hundred slaves including the leader, Prince Klaas (aka King Court Tackey)

1807 Abolition of the slave trade

1834 Emancipation. Britain's Slavery Abolition Act comes into force

1860 Barbuda 'ownership' reverts to the British crown

1871-1956 Antigua and Barbuda administered together as part of the Leeward Islands Federation

1899 Parham ceases to be capital of Antigua

1900 St John's becomes the capital of Antigua

1939 Antigua Trades and Labour Union formed

1946 Vere Cornwall (V.C.) Bird forms the Antigua Labour Party (ALP)

1951 Antigua Labour Party wins first general election under universal adult suffrage.

1958-1962 Antigua and Barbuda part of the short-lived West Indies Federation

1960 Vere C. Bird sworn in as the country's first Chief Minister

1965 Caribbean Free Trade Association (CARIFTA) founded

1967 Antigua and Barbuda becomes a self-governing state within the British Commonwealth

1967 V.C. Bird sworn in as the country's first Premier

1971 Progressive Labour Movement (PLM) wins the general election. George H. Walter becomes the country's second Premier

1972 Sugar industry closed down

1976 ALP wins general election. V.C. Bird re-appointed Premier

1981 Antigua and Barbuda gains Independence from Great Britain and also becomes a member of the Commonwealth of Nations

1994 V.C. Bird resigns as Prime Minister and is replaced by his son, Lester

1994 ALP wins general election. Lester Bird elected as Prime Minister

1995 Hurricane Luis devastates Antigua and Barbuda

1999 ALP wins general election. Lester Bird re-elected as Prime Minister

2004 ALP loses general election. Baldwin Spencer, leader of the United Progressive Party (UPP), elected as Prime Minister

2007 Dame Louise A. Lake-Tack becomes the country's first female Governor-General

2009 UPP wins general election. Baldwin Spencer re-elected as Prime Minister

2014 Antigua and Barbuda Labour Party (ABLP), formerly ALP, wins general election. Gaston Browne elected as Prime Minister

2014 Sir Rodney E. Williams sworn in as Governor-General

"Open invitation to visit a little bit of paradise."

INTRODUCTION

There are hundreds of reasons to visit Antigua and Barbuda, and not just for the 365 beaches, although this would be a good place to start. Nothing feels more like paradise than immersing yourself in the clear, aquamarine waters of a tropical sea, or feeling the powder-soft sand between your toes, or simply relaxing in the shade of a coconut tree. These are some of the key elements of the quintessential Caribbean beach scene and, some might say, reasons enough to visit 'Paradise on Earth'. But, Antigua and Barbuda has so much more to offer, you only have to take a closer look ... and consider ten more reasons.

One – Carnival: The pageantry and pan, and the calypso and creativity of Carnival is held in late July to early August and is a vibrant celebration of Antiguan and Barbudan culture, history and artistry. From the thumping bass of the music to the dazzling colours of the mas parades, few can resist the intoxicating sights, sounds and rhythms of this spectacular occasion.

Two – Mother Nature: Blessed with warm, tropical sunshine, soothing trade winds, crystal-clear waters and lush vegetation, Antigua and Barbuda truly is a little bit of paradise. Here, you can swim with stingrays, spot a hawksbill sea turtle or witness a breaching whale at sea; or, on land, hike the Shekerly Hills to Mount Obama, or Wallings Dam to Signal Hill; or explore the offshore islands, including Great Bird Island, home to the world's rarest and most harmless snake – the Antiguan racer.

Three – Sailing: Antigua and Barbuda plays host to a number of sailing events that attract participants from across the globe. One such event, Antigua Sailing Week, is now in its 48th year and is the Caribbean's oldest regatta. Other events include the Antigua Classic Regatta and the Super Yacht Challenge. To accommodate these events, Antigua offers world class marinas and marine services, particularly at English Harbour.

Four – Cosmopolitan: Located towards the south-eastern end of the Leeward Islands chain, Antigua and Barbuda is well-positioned to also serve as a hub for the Windward Islands as well as the wider Caribbean. With its new terminal, V.C. Bird International Airport is now the largest airport in the Leeward Islands and handles nearly one million passengers every year. The country's main seaport is in the capital, St John's, and can accommodate four cruise ships at a time. Responding to these 'cruise ship days', the surrounding quay has

Galleon Beach, English
Harbour / JJ

become a popular shopping centre for local crafts, souvenirs and duty free goods. A wide selection of hotels, from small boutiques to the most luxurious, makes Antigua and Barbuda an attractive destination for tourists and businesspeople from across the globe.

Five – Food: Fungee, pepperpot, rice pudding, ducana and saltfish, goat water, and old-school wood-oven bread are local favourites. And because of the country's cosmopolitan nature, many restaurants, cafes and bars serve up some of the tastiest food from around the Caribbean and across the world... with a distinctive local touch.

Six – Mangoes: In fact, lots of tropical fruit, from sweet soursop to the even sweeter sugar apple, from guinep to guava, and the distinctive Antigua black pineapple. But the mango, especially, is showcased during the popular annual Mango Festival that includes a 'mixologist' and chef competition, as if this unofficial summer fruit in its natural state wasn't already a feast for the palate.

Seven – History: Colonial era buildings and architecture, including military fortifications, slave dungeons, sugar mills and churches, speak volumes about Antigua and Barbuda's cultural and social history. Nelson's Dockyard, for example, is named after Britain's naval hero,

Admiral Horatio Nelson, who was stationed in Antigua in the 1780s.

Eight – Size: At only 108 square miles for Antigua, and 62 square miles for Barbuda, the twin-island nation is easy to navigate – whether by organised tour or rental vehicle, bus, taxi, motorbike, bicycle or on foot. Antigua and Barbuda is a place where you can wander freely but are never lost.

Nine – Sporting Legends: In cricket alone, Antigua is home to Sir Vivian Richards, Sir Andy Roberts, Sir Curtly Ambrose and Sir Richie Richardson. For cricket fans, time here could mean a sighting of these and other greats who made their name on the pitch and who serve as examples of the big-hearted will of Antiguan and Barbudan people.

Ten – Wadadli: This is the modern transliteration of the name given to Antigua by the indigenous Arawak peoples (Barbuda's name is Wa'omani). Today, the name is branded into many things, most notably, Wadadli Beer, an essential ingredient when 'liming' (hanging out).

These are just ten more reasons to visit Antigua and Barbuda but they, and the following pages, serve as an open invitation to come to this little bit of paradise and experience it for yourself.

Barbuda is renowned for its miles of deserted beaches / Photo Alexander Shalamov

Old Road village at Carlisle Bay / JJ

Palm Beach at Low Bay on the Caribbean Sea side of Codrington Lagoon in Barbuda / JJ

Rendezvous Bay / JJ

Ffryes Beach / JJ

Morris Bay / JJ

Pigeon Beach in Falmouth Bay / JJ

Codrington Lagoon in Barbuda / JJ

Super yachts moored at Falmouth Harbour for the Charter Yacht Show / JJ

St John's harbour can accommodate up to four cruise ships at a time and any number of small fishing boats / JJ

Windward Bay / JJ

Antigua's coastline is a series of coves
and tranquil bays / Photo Paul Zizka

Jennings Village seen from McNish Mountain in the parish of St Mary / JJ

View across Falmouth Harbour / Photo Guppyimages

Galleon Beach / JJ

Morris Bay / JJ

Antigua's many beaches offer peace and tranquillity / Photo Linda Johnsonbaugh

The Ffryes Beach at Ffryes Bay / JJ

Ffryes Beach / JJ

Valley Church Bay / JJ

Yachts seen from Windward Bay / JJ

Coco Point Beach in Barbuda / JJ

A typical Antiguan vista / Photo Sergey Kelin

Traditional-style accommodation / Photo Jgorzynik-Dreamstime

Tyrell's located near All Saints village / JJ

Native to the Windward Islands, the agave is the national flower of Antigua and Barbuda. It is also known as dagger log or batta log (in Barbuda), or century plant. It flowers once in 10 to 20 years then it dies, hence its other name, century plant. It can grow to a height of around 18 ft and its dagger-like, sharp-tipped leaves grow up to 3 ft in length / JJ

Curtain Bluff Resort at Carlisle Bay / Photo Sergey Kelin

Unspoilt Barbuda / Photo Schoolgirl-Dreamstime

"Paradise on Earth."

BARBUDA

Antigua and Barbuda is known as a little bit of paradise, but the island of Barbuda, itself, really does have *all* the qualities of paradise on Earth – peace, seclusion, mile after mile of unspoilt beaches, crystal-clear waters and tranquil lagoons.

Located 28 miles north of its sister island, and occupying 62 sq miles, Barbuda has its own character. Where the twin-island nation is known for its white-sand beaches, Barbuda is also renowned for its pink sand; the hue caused by tiny shells and crushed coral mixing with the white sand. And life in Barbuda moves at a slower pace and its people are famed for their warmth and friendliness, the majority of whom live in Codrington, the island's main town.

Europeans first settled in 1666 and, later, the island was leased to Englishmen, Christopher

Barbuda is renowned for its pink-sand beaches / Alexander Shalamov

The view from one of Barbuda's caves / Photo Schoolgirl-Dreamstime

The Martello Tower is a reminder of Barbuda's colonial past / JJ

and John Codrington for an initial fifty years in 1685 for the fee of "one fat sheep on demand". Additional leases granted them salvage rights to the ships that were wrecked on the island's coral reefs. The Codringtons resided at Highland House, built c1720 and now in ruins.

Located on the south coast near River Landing, the Martello Tower is a dominant edifice that is another reminder of Barbuda's colonial past. It was built by the British in the early 19th century and would have housed three cannons offering protection to the quay at River Landing. The tower is attached to the remains of the pre-existing fort and is the highest building on the island.

For the more adventurous holidaymaker, Barbuda offers a range of natural wonders, including three caves of note to explore. Located at Two Foot Bay on the rugged north-eastern coast, Indian Cave is the site of a number of Amerindian petroglyphs (rock drawings). Two miles south of Indian Cave is Dark Cave, which runs for 400 feet and is home

to rock pools, bats and the rare blind eye shrimp. Darby's Sink Cave is located about three miles from Codrington and is approximately 350 feet in diameter and 70 feet deep. It is characterised by the rich vegetation growing on its interior walls giving it a 'lost world' appearance. The sheltered nature of the sink-hole has given rise to a luxuriant micro-climate of tropical flora and fauna. Together with an array of stalactites and stalagmites, this hidden gem is an essential stopover for any visitor to Barbuda.

Codrington Lagoon is home to one of the world's largest colonies of magnificent frigate birds. The lagoon occupies most of the north-western region of the island and is an official wetlands conservation area.

Once home to Amerindian communities, Spanish Point, on the south-eastern coast, is defined by its rugged terrain, coastal bays, crashing Atlantic waves and the mystery of shipwrecks beneath the waves. As well providing a habitat for a spectacular array of marine life, the reefs are also the resting places of around 120 ill-fated ships of a bygone era.

For many years, Barbuda has attracted the rich and famous, including the late Princess Diana, for whom Barbuda was an annual holiday destination during the 1980s and 1990s. The pink-sand beach at the former K Club resort, on the southern tip of the island, was renamed Princess Diana Beach in 2011, the year in which she would have turned fifty.

In 2015, a US $250m investment to redevelop 251 acres at Coco Point, on the abandoned site of the former K Club, was agreed. Headed by Hollywood actor Robert de Niro and billionaire Australian James Packer, the project will be managed by Paradise Resorts and the new development will be named Paradise Found.

For some, it seems that paradise has now been found. However, it is hoped that this little bit of paradise will not be lost to those who call it home.

Joanne C. Hillhouse

Codrington Lagoon National Park runs along Barbuda's west coast and is home to one of the world's largest colonies of frigate birds / Photo Schoolgirl-Dreamstime

"Something for everyone."

A DAY OUT IN ANTIGUA AND BARBUDA

Antigua and Barbuda has a little something for everyone: whether environmentally conscious, adventurous, favouring lazy days on the beach or just 'liming', as the locals say. For those cruising through, with only a day or less to spend, it can still be an unforgettable experience.

Essential stops in the capital include the Antigua and Barbuda Museum, which used to be the Court House during the 18th century. The museum displays many historical items as well as a selection of pre-Columbian artefacts. A short walk up the road takes strollers to the beautiful St John's Anglican Cathedral that dominates the city's skyline with its imposing twin towers.

At the bottom of 'town' are the shopping centres of Heritage Quay and Redcliffe Quay, both of which are ideal for souvenir hunters. Redcliffe Quay has several small stores that have the characteristics and infrastructure of an older St John's, whereas Heritage Quay has more modern buildings and a vendors' market from where trinkets, t-shirts and other Antiguan and Barbudan keepsakes may be purchased.

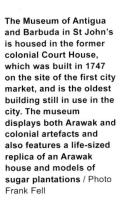

The Museum of Antigua and Barbuda in St John's is housed in the former colonial Court House, which was built in 1747 on the site of the first city market, and is the oldest building still in use in the city. The museum displays both Arawak and colonial artefacts and also features a life-sized replica of an Arawak house and models of sugar plantations / Photo Frank Fell

St John's Anglican Cathedral is located in the capital and is the seat of the Diocese of the North East Caribbean and Aruba in the Church in the Province of the West Indies / Photo Frank Fell

Interior of St John's Cathedral / JJ

The area is also dotted with a number of small restaurants and bars offering a wide selection of mouth-watering dishes, both local and international.

Beyond St John's is Devil's Bridge, a rocky, coastal location on the eastern-most side of the island facing the Atlantic Ocean. Here, the sea crashes against the 'bridge' and shoots huge sprays up through the blowhole.

A popular detour along the route is Betty's Hope, a former sugarcane plantation that was established in the mid-17th century. A programme of restoration was implemented in the early 1990s and it has since served as an open-air museum and visitor centre.

Also of historical note are Shirley Heights Lookout and Nelson's Dockyard, both located at the southern tip of Antigua. Shirley Heights is a former military complex and signal station (or 'lookout') which has a number of historic ruins and renovated buildings serving both as a museum and popular dining and entertainment venue. Its elevated position also offers spectacular views of English Harbour. Nelson's Dockyard, in English Harbour itself and named after Britain's Admiral Horatio Nelson, is a cultural heritage site and marina. It is home to historic naval buildings that date back to the 18th century, and the Dockyard Museum.

Galleon Beach, also in English Harbour, is popular with locals and tourists alike.

For a more natural experience, one might take a lazy drive through the beautiful rainforest of Fig Tree Drive. And another good beach stop on this south-west-heading route is Callaloo Bay, which is one of the few beaches still lined with coconut trees.

Villages along this route include Old Road and Urlings, and into Johnson's Point, where Mrs Turner, of Turner's Beach Bar, turns her hand to local delights such as conch fritters, grilled lobster, barbeque ribs and curry chicken. The bar is on the beach and is a temptation to all who come to swim, sunbathe or just relax and soak-up the quintessentially Caribbean location. It is also the perfect spot from which to see the setting sun, drawing to a close yet another day in paradise.

Sally Davis

Pigeon Beach / JJ

Betty's Hope was a sugarcane plantation in Antigua and was established in 1650, shortly after the island had become an English colony. It was the first large-scale sugar plantation to operate in Antigua and belonged to the Codrington family from 1674 until 1944. Christopher Codrington, later Captain General of the Leeward Islands, acquired the property in 1674 and named it Betty's Hope, after his daughter / JJ

EXOTIC ANTIGUA
DUTY FREE
HARBOUR VIEW BAR & CAFÉ

Treasure Island Cruises

St John's Harbour / Photo Irishka777-Dreamstime

Turner's Beach / JJ

Sea Cloud is a sailing cruise ship of the Sea Cloud Cruises line. Initially built as a private yacht, it subsequently served as a weather ship for the US Coast Guard and US Navy during World War II. The ship served as the first racially integrated warship in the US Armed Forces since the American Civil War. Following the war, Sea Cloud was returned to private ownership, serving as a yacht for numerous people, including as presidential yacht of the Dominican Republic. The ship currently sails in Europe and the Caribbean as part of a fleet of sail cruise ships operated by Sea Cloud Cruises / Photo Linda Johnsonbaugh

The yellow pui tree, pictured at the Hall's Estate, and was brought to the island from Trinidad / JJ

Falmouth Harbour is a horseshoe-shaped natural harbour in the south of Antigua. The small township of Falmouth lies close to its northern shore, and English Harbour is located close to its eastern shore / Photo Robert Lerich

Carlisle Bay / JJ

The Antigua and Barbuda International Kite Festival is held at Easter at Devil's Bridge / JJ

Redcliffe Quay / JJ

Fishing boats at St John's wharf and fish market / JJ

CARIBBEAN PRINCESS

Cruise ship passengers disembark to savour the delights of duty free shopping in St John's / JJ

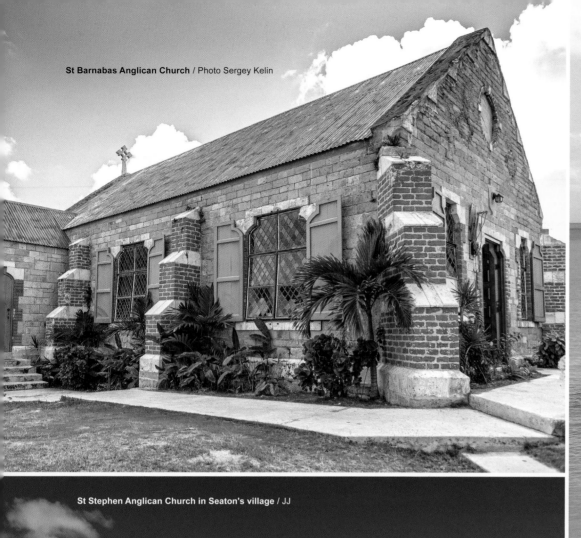

St Barnabas Anglican Church / Photo Sergey Kelin

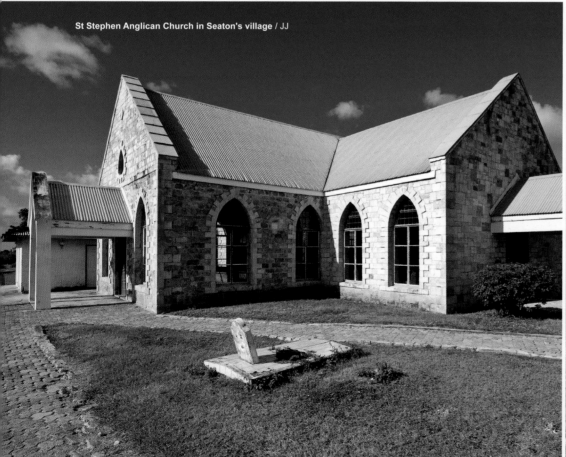

St Stephen Anglican Church in Seaton's village / JJ

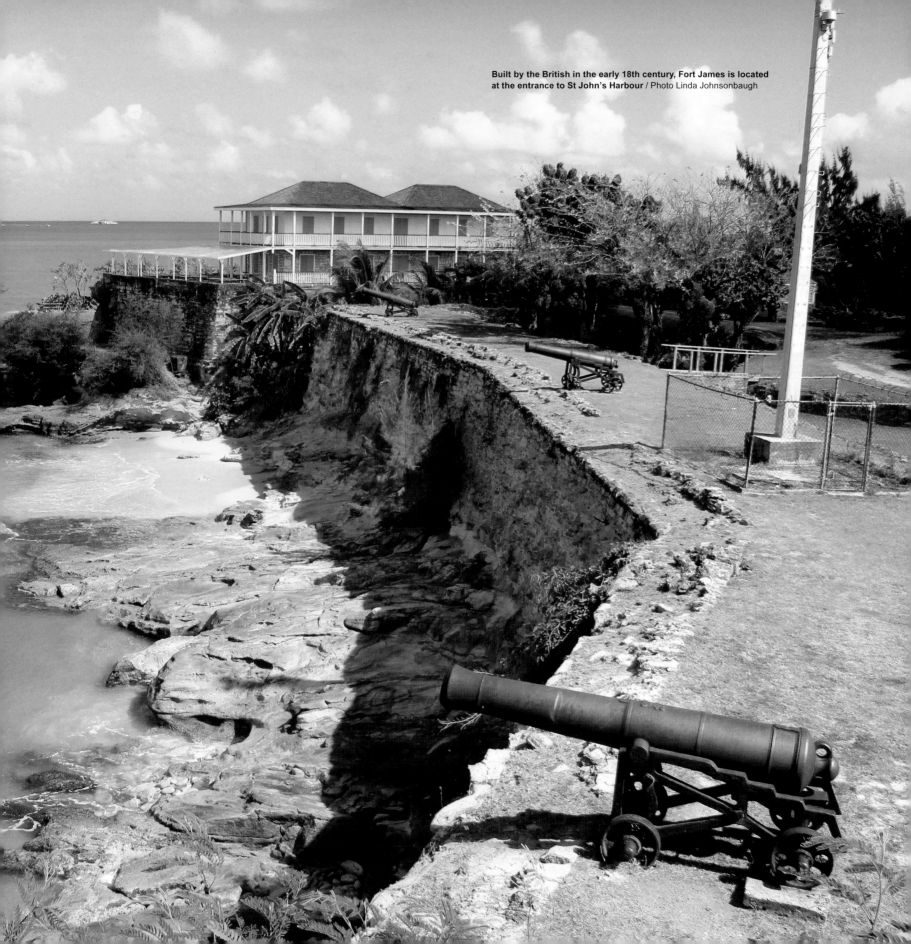

Built by the British in the early 18th century, Fort James is located at the entrance to St John's Harbour / Photo Linda Johnsonbaugh

Candy Land is a popular beach bar and restaurant near Fort James in St John's Harbour / JJ

Clemie's fruit and vegetable stall in Old Road on Fig Tree Drive / JJ

Jabberwock Beach at Judge's Bay
on Antigua's north coast / JJ

Sandals Grande Antigua Resort & Spa at Dickenson Bay / JJ

Verandah Resort & Spa at Mercers Creek Bay / Photo Boris Hudak

Ffryes Beach / JJ

Turner's Beach Bar and Restaurant / JJ

The Siboney Beach Club is an intimate resort located at Dickenson Bay. It is set within luxuriant tropical gardens and is noted for its attentive and friendly staff / Photo courtesy Siboney Beach Club

"Sit back and enjoy the ride!"

ANTIGUA AND BARBUDA BY BUS

Call it an adventure and not a journey, because a journey is usually predictable and an adventure may be anything but. And that is what it feels like when travelling by bus in Antigua and Barbuda.

To begin with, waiting for a bus may take minutes or even hours – whether standing at a bus stop in the tranquil countryside or sitting in a bus waiting for it to leave one of the capital's vibrant bus stations.

But what kind of bus? One of the older ones with worn and torn upholstery and temperamental door handles; perhaps a newer one with dark tinted windows that beckon passengers to an environment of air-conditioned luxury; or a bus that is somewhere in between? Whichever you choose, you *will* get from A to B ... eventually!

And what about the bus driver? Some are well suited to the job and carry out their duties with distinction. Some, however, are better suited for the racetrack as they swerve in and out of traffic in an attempt to 'get there first'. Then there are the silent types who only speak when spoken to; and there are those who are the talkers, with an opinion on anything and everything.

But the bus driver is only one of the many characters on this adventure through paradise.

Others include the elderly woman in the front row with a bag almost too big for public transport and bursting at the seams with purchases from the local market – fruit, vegetables, fish or spices; the security guard on his way to work, his over-pressed uniform shimmering in the sunlight; fractious babies and their frustrated mothers; adventurous toddlers with a determination to explore; excitable schoolchildren and their reticent peers; and the eager tourists on a day-trip to wherever. All of them embarking on a journey together.

Then there are the unscheduled stops; the detour to drop a passenger at their front door, or the speculative drive down a side-street looking for anyone 'going to town'.

Regular bus travellers soon learn not to leave anything to chance: arrive at the bus stop early, be ready to move at a moment's notice and have the exact bus fare to hand.

While the bus service may be fraught with unpredictability, and timetables mere dreams and wishes, all that remains is to sit back, take in the sights and sounds of Antigua and Barbuda, and enjoy the ride.

Kimolisa Mings

Catching a bus at Urlings village / JJ

THE PARISHES OF ANTIGUA AND BARBUDA

The six parishes of Antigua are: St John, St George, St Peter, St Philip, St Paul and St Mary. Off mainland Antigua, there are the administrative divisions (dependencies) of Barbuda and Redonda.

ST GEORGE
Capital: Piggots
Sites of interest: St George's Anglican Church in Fitches Creek, one of the oldest churches in Antigua, built in 1687; V.C. Bird International Airport, named after the country's first Prime Minister ('Father of the Nation') Sir Vere Cornwall Bird Sr.; Sea View Farm, located in the middle of the island is famous for its pottery tradition as practiced by Elvie's Pottery, the oldest of its kind, where coal pots and other items are made of clay using a traditional method handed down through generations of women; New Winthorpes village, relocated in 1942 to make room for the construction of the nearby US base.

ST JOHN
Capital: St John's
Sites of interest: St John's Cathedral, with statues of St John the Divine and St John the Baptist, lifted from a French ship during the Seven Years' War at the Temple Street graveyard entrance; Viv Richards and Andy Roberts streets in Ovals, named after two of the greatest Antiguan-born cricketers of all time; the Westerby Memorial, bottom of High Street, in memory of Moravian Bishop Westerby, who was instrumental in providing education to formerly enslaved Africans and improving the water supply in St John's; Government House,

the Georgian-era building is the official seat of the Governor-General; Cenotaph, unveiled 1919, is a war memorial for those Antiguans and Barbudans who died in the two World Wars; St John's Market and site of a statue honouring Sir V.C. Bird Sr.; a statue of world famous cricketer and national hero Sir Vivian Richards can be found at the cricket stadium named after him; St John's Botanical Garden, originally created in 1893, a major feature is the more than eighty-year-old African cloth bark tree or Zulu tree which is about 40 feet high; the old Courthouse, the oldest building in town, circa 1750, now houses the museum; the stone at the corner of Newgate and Popeshead Streets, placed there during the Emancipation celebrations of 1984; Fort James, named after King James II, today a popular beach and site of one of the oldest (at more than 300 years) colonial fortifications; Fort Barrington on Goat Hill above Deep Bay.

ST MARY
Capital: Bolans
Sites of interest: Greencastle Hill or, as described in a 1971 article in the *New York Times*, "Antigua's Tropical Stonehenge", where 565 feet up there are megaliths believed to be of prehistoric astrological significance; Wallings, a forest, dam and reservoir built between 1890 and 1897 and is an ideal bird-watching and hiking location; rock dungeon at Orange Valley, downward from the western slope of Mount Obama, that was used to punish enslaved Africans; Fig Tree Hill, a winding drive through the most verdant part of the country.

ST PAUL

Capital: Falmouth

Sites of interest: Bat's Cave, owned by Colonel Philip Warner back in 1676 and considered a valuable natural resource for the gunpowder ingredient, saltpetre, extracted from the bat guano found there; Nelson's Dockyard National Park, where you'll find fortifications (including the ones at Monk's Hill and Fort Berkeley) and colonial era buildings including the dockyard, named after Britain's Admiral Horatio Nelson, which is now the only working Georgian era naval yard in the world and now a World Heritage Site; the Pillars of Hercules, where erosion over time on the eastern side of English harbour has carved an interesting rock formation; Shirley Heights Lookout, once a colonial era military complex named after one-time Governor of the Leeward Islands, Sir Thomas Shirley, now one of the island's favoured Sunday liming spots and from where the country's most iconic vista may be seen - English Harbour; Bethesda Tamarind Tree, pivotal meeting point between sugar barons and striking workers during the year-long 1951 strike.

ST PETER

Capital: Parham

Sites of interest: Parham town which is historically significant as the main town and shipping point for sugar, and residence of the Lt. Governor Colonel Christopher Codrington, before it was eclipsed by St John's City in the 1700s; St Peter's Anglican Church, built 1840, is a historical church of note for both its age and unique architecture; Potworks, the island's main water catchment, named after the skilled Black potters who once worked the area making conical sugar pots for draining molasses from raw sugar – the reservoir was opened in 1970, covers 320 acres, and has a capacity of one billion gallons of water when full.

ST PHILIP

Capital: Carlisle

Sites of interest: Betty's Hope, named after Joan Elizabeth, wife of the first owner, Governor Keynell, was the island's oldest sugar plantation – most identified with the Codrington family to which it was granted in 1674, it is now an open air museum; Devil's Bridge on the eastern ridge of the island and, according to local folklore, is a site where enslaved Africans jumped to their death. It is a natural wonder of eroded rock shaped by the Atlantic Ocean. The area is also the location of the annual Easter Monday Kite Festival.

BARBUDA

Capital: Codrington

Sites of interest: Caves (Dark Cave, Darby's Cave, Indian Cave) features of which, respectively, include the blind shrimp, stalagmites and Amerindian petroglyphs; the lagoon with mangroves and the Frigate Bird Sanctuary; historical relics like the 'castle' and Martello Tower, both used for defence during the colonial era; Spanish Point, the south-easterly region of the island where Amerindians settled about 500 CE; shipwrecks – various ships, including slave ships, have been wrecked over the centuries amid the reefs; the ruins of former Codrington residence, built sometime after 1720, Highland House, known locally as Willybob; long stretches of pink-sand beach including Princess Diana Beach, named after the late British Princess for whom Barbuda was a favourite vacation spot.

REDONDA

Sites of interest: Centaur's Cave, an abandoned mine. Other offshore islands include Guiana, Hell's Gate, Maiden and Great Bird, the site of one of the world's rarest snakes, the Antiguan racer.

St. John's Cathedral / JJ

St John's Harbour / Photo Irishka777-Dreamstime

Cruise ship port in St John's Harbour / Photo Kennethchern

Sunset at Morris Bay / JJ

Shoul's Toy, Gifts & Housewares in St John's was founded in 1974 by John F. Shoul and his son David. This family business is well known for its annual sale in October which heralds the start of Christmas shopping in Antigua and Barbuda. The late Sir John Ferdinand Shoul was the first Chairman of the Antigua Carnival and first Chairman of the Tourism Board. Ambassador David Shoul is recognised for building a greater relationship with the People's Republic of China. He is now Antigua and Barbuda's Ambassador to the Holy See / Photo courtesy Shoul's

Children at the Foundation Mixed School / JJ

St John's Market / JJ

Budding footballers at Trinity Academy / JJ

A game of cards in Freetown / JJ

Local fashion designers display their creations at the annual Independence Fashion Show / JJ

Independence Food Fair / JJ

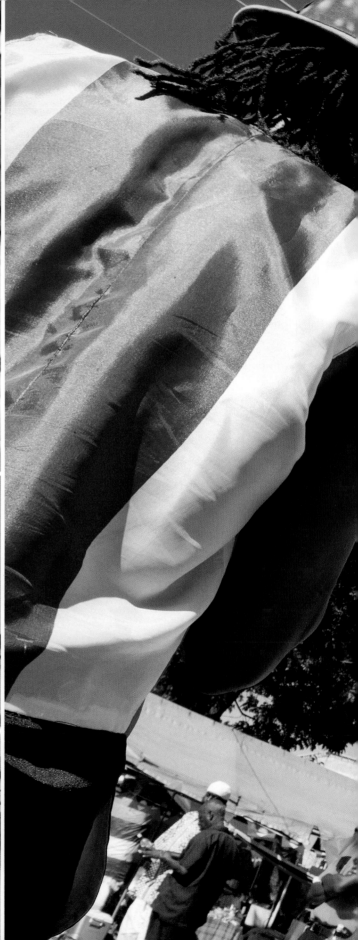

Aunty Esther takes on a challenger in a game of
Warri, a traditional Antiguan board game / JJ

Personal beachfront service / JJ

A young customer at Wag's Barbershop on Bendals Road / JJ

A relaxing afternoon
at Cades Bay / JJ

Kite Festival at Devil's Bridge / JJ

Pathfinders March of Witness through Five Islands. Pathfinders is a worldwide organisation of young people sponsored by the Seventh-day Adventist Church / JJ

Youth Rally during Independence celebrations / JJ

Independnce Ceremonial Parade / JJ

The Foundation Mixed School is one of Antigua's oldest private grade schools / JJ

"Investing in today's youth for a brighter future."

EDUCATION

The average day for a young person in Antigua and Barbuda starts with the early morning preparation for the school day. Education is mandatory up to the age of sixteen and all public schools are free. There are over seventy public and private schools in the twin-island nation, including two institutions for children with disabilities.

At the end of the school day, many children attend one of a number of sporting hubs: the YMCA in St John's has basketball, netball and volleyball courts; while the YASCO sporting facility, just outside the city, attracts primarily footballers and track and field athletes. Cricket youth teams, meanwhile, converge at the Rising Sun Sports grounds. For those not located in town, nearly every village has its own basketball, football and cricket pitch.

After graduating from secondary school, most students make their way to a number of tertiary institutions. Probably the most well-known is the Antigua State College, which has a number of departments for those wishing to further their studies, including the Advanced Level Department and the Departments of Business, Engineering, Teacher Education and

After secondary school, most students make their way to a tertiary institution / JJ

Youth Rally during Independence celebrations / JJ

Nursing. There is also the opportunity to pursue full-time studies with the University of the West Indies (UWI), Department of Undergraduate Studies, which allows students to do years one and two of a full degree program in Antigua, before finishing at a UWI campus in Barbados, Jamaica or Trinidad.

Other tertiary education opportunities include the Antigua and Barbuda Institute for Continuing Studies, which provides vocational and skills training; and the Antigua and Barbuda International Institute of Technology which offers a number of accredited business and design programs and is also affiliated with overseas colleges and universities such as Monroe College and Midwestern State University in the United States.

Antigua and Barbuda is also home to two medical universities: the University of Health Sciences Antigua and the American University of Antigua, both of which have a large number of American students.

Tertiary education is also supported with government scholarships, grants and low interest loans for those who need financial assistance to pursue studies overseas.

Youth outreach programmes, meanwhile, are run through the Department of Youth Affairs, which implemented a National Youth Policy in 2007 that sets out guidelines for overall youth development.

Antigua and Barbuda's prospects are closely linked to how it educates and develops the youth of today. The challenge, therefore, is for it to continue to invest in them so that the future will be as bright as the Caribbean sun.

Daryl George

114

Youth Rally during Independence celebrations / JJ

Local fashion designers display their creations
at the annual Independence Fashion Show / JJ

"A wealth of creativity."

THE ARTS

Cultural expression in Antigua and Barbuda has changed over the decades – in the 1970s theatre ruled; now it is dance, film, spoken word, visual artists and pop-up creative events.

Vibrant movements open to all are redefining what to expect from artists living and working in the Caribbean.

Visual arts output includes traditional paintings that capture the island's natural beauty and portraits of famous individuals and everyday day people; the range – modern, mixed media to graffiti influenced works. Although there is no national art gallery, works can be seen at individual galleries including, Harmony Hall, Zemi (Stephen Murphy), Gilly Gobinet's Calypso Graphics, Sally Harker's Fig Tree studio and by contacting individual artists through social media. Mark Brown, Dina de Brozzi, Anson J. Henry, Heather Doram, Emille Hill, Maritza Martin, Guava De Artist, Lyris Tracy and Charmaine B. Werth are just a few of Antigua and Barbuda's contemporary artists.

These artists explore their world and present another way of seeing beauty. Some utilise nature to produce items from shells, driftwood, beach-finds, wood, calabash

An artistic welcome to Green Bay / JJ

Traditional pottery made by Hyacinth Hillhouse / JJ

(gourd), coconut, sea glass, clay and reclaimed items.

The traditional red clay utility pots made primarily by Sea View Farm potters may not be as popular as they were when they were a functional part of daily life, but red clay and white clay are being used by potters and ceramicists to make bold pieces – light fixtures, garden sculptures, figurines, jewellery, table and kitchenware and commissioned pieces. Hyacinth Hillhouse (Elvie's Pottery), Nancy Nicholson (Rhythm of Blue), Michael and Imogen Hunte (Cedars Pottery) and Sarah Fuller (Pottery Shop) are examples of people doing this type of work.

In fashion, our local designers create pieces fit for daily or event wear that are as artistic as anything found hanging on a wall. Many jewellers utilise local materials – sea glass, wood, coconut, semi-precious jewels. The Goldsmitty, for one, has been creating organic gold jewellery for over two decades. Antiguanite is one of their keystones and, as the name suggests, it can only be found in Antigua. Meanwhile, Miranda Askie's big, bold, vibrant pieces in semi-precious stones, calabash, leather and copper are as individual as the designer; while her bags and clothing are tapestries of fabric, wood and leather. Young

Wally Jackson produces handmade souvenirs at his workshop in Liberta Village and sells them at a location opposote St Barnabas Church / JJ

High quality, locally-made leather goods / JJ

jewellery makers are also popular at fairs organised by churches and social groups. Independence (celebrated in November) is a great time for such local fairs.

Talk of fashion in Antigua would be incomplete without the name, Calvin S, who has designed for individuals locally, regionally and internationally. His artistry is given full flow during the annual Carnival celebrations, where art meets Mas and storytelling. In addition to event pageants, he designs for his own 'Beautiful People Mas' which has grown from a group of friends to over 300 strong. Space also has to be made in the conversation for another

veteran of the Antiguan fashion scene, Noreen Philips, whose clients know that when they shop at her Redcliffe Quay boutique, they are buying wearable art – flowing sheaths and bejewelled evening/cocktail gowns, colour and prints designed by Noreen. Up and coming designers also get to show their style at local fashion competitions like Courts' annual Young designers competition, usually late summer, in which the designers are given a mandate to create clothes that reflect the fashion of interior design.

Spoken word artistes, meanwhile, are flourishing under the spotlight of the rising popularity of performance poetry, which has

National Youth Choir of Antigua and Barbuda / JJ

spawned events like Expressions: Poetry in the Pub (second Tuesday of every month, September to June, Heavenly Java in Redcliffe Quay), Wadadli Pen Open Mic (second Saturday, the Best of Books on St Mary's Street) and Soothe (March, Splash Antigua at Fort James) – the latter featuring jazz and spoken word.

Dance groups – Antigua Dance Academy (folk Caribbean), the Dance Centre (ballet), Shiva's School of Dance (fusion) – put on annual productions (usually early summer); and, year-round, contemporary to ballroom (Terpsichorean Ballroom Dancers) to African dance are all practiced here. Drumming and

exquisite costumes are signatures of several of the local productions.

Where there's dance, there's music and while reggae, soca and calypso are synonymous with island music vibes, one can periodically find classical, jazz and pan shows (a highlight of which is the Gemonites Moods of Pan in late November) – with performances by local and regional artistes.

In Antigua and Barbuda, the beach is really just the beginning; cultural expression and events are open to all to learn, embrace and enjoy.

Brenda Lee Browne

123

The pageantry of Carnival is Antigua and Barbuda's most striking artform / JJ

A RICH LITERARY TRADITION

Though a very young nation, Antigua and Barbuda boasts a vibrant literary tradition with long-established roots, claiming 18th and 19th century writers like Rev. William Shervington, Rebecca Freundlich and sisters Elizabeth Hart Thwaites and Anne Hart Gilbert. There is also the curious case of Freida Cassin's 19th century novel, *With Silent Tread* (published around 1888-1892), believed to be the oldest Antiguan and Barbudan novel. Previously neglected, Cassin's novel was reprinted in 2002 in the Macmillan Caribbean Classic Series and is fascinating in its presentation of Antiguan-English on page and its interrogation of post-emancipation Antiguan society.

Today, more than a century after Cassin (who also edited one of Antigua's earliest literary journals *The Carib*), Antigua and Barbuda's prose tradition attracts much critical attention. This is due in large part to the prolific output of the nation's most well-known writer, Jamaica Kincaid, whose first book, *At the Bottom of the River*, appeared in 1983. The internationally acclaimed Kincaid, a controversial figure locally, is best known for her explorations of literal and symbolic mother-daughter relationships that are rife with tensions. She also exhibits a penchant for novels heavily reliant on autobiographical and historical details as well as experimentations with narrative forms and techniques.

The nation's ever-growing canon has also benefited significantly from the inputs of authors such as Joanne C. Hillhouse, Ashley Bryan, D. Gisele Isaac, Edgar Lake, Althea Prince, Marie-Elena John and Dorbrene E. O'Marde. The offerings of these writers not only elaborate themes familiar to Caribbean literature. They also engage in the necessary act of articulating and inserting new/neglected subjectivities and perspectives that query local, regional and international realities.

The nation's poetic tradition, too, has benefited from important contributions ranging from the humorous verses of poets like Sylvanus Barnes to Veronica Evanson Bernard's early use of Antiguan-English, to Clifton Joseph's and Iyaba Ibo Mandigo's dub poetry's petition against the conventional snubbing of oral literary traditions. Also not to be forgotten are playwrights, such as Dorbrene O'Marde (Harambee Open-Air Theatre), Eleston Adams (the Rio Revellers Theatre), and Leon Symester (The Third World Theatre), whose theatre houses regularly toured the Caribbean and internationally in the 20th century.

With the investment of these and other scribes in genres such as romance, comedic verse, illustrated children's books and more, Antiguan and Barbudan writers exhibit a ready willingness to resist the too-neat categorisations that insist Caribbean poetry, prose and drama ought to be solid examples of literary fiction, "serious" political/social commentaries and the like. The "local" section of the island's bookshops is bound to surprise.

Dr Hazra Medica

"A time of flamboyant egalitarian fervour."

CARNIVAL IN ANTIGUA AND BARBUDA

Famed Antiguan calypsonian, King Short Shirt, in his 1980 ode to Carnival, *Summer Festival*, dubbed the event, "the Caribbean's most colourful". And regardless of what any other Carnival promoter anywhere else says, locals still testify that Antigua's is the best.

Established in 1957, and celebrating its Diamond Jubilee in 2017, Antigua's Carnival runs for about ten days, ending on the first Tuesday in August. The organisers, whose first Chairman was 'Ferdi' Shoul, were mainly from the business community and seized the opportunity to stimulate economic activity by creating a summer tourist attraction. Over time, they found a marriage with the cultural staples of what was then the main celebration at the Yuletide season, and thus it began. This is where Carnival still resides: at the junction of culture and commerce.

A variety of shows constitute the festival's line-up, with music, dance, costumes, pageantry and performance as the heartbeat.

Carnival Queen
contestants in 1964

126

The Parade of Troupes / JJ

Panorama Competition / JJ

The Parade of Troupes on Carnival Tuesday / JJ

The Calypso Monarch Competition is a main feature. Once the preserve of men as the original Calypso King title reminds, this contest whittles down an average of seventy aspirants each year to just nine to face the titleholder. Yesteryear, when the party tunes (the road march) were provided by calypsonians, they sang a commentary song and a party song in the two-round contest. These days, depending on the contender, you can get two serious songs, two jumpy ones, or one of each. What's certain is that there is bound to be stinging commentaries; locals know well that, if a politician runs afoul of the masses during the year, calypso will call their name. This is the competition that gave to the world King Short Shirt (Sir Mclean Emanuel), Swallow (Sir Rupert Philo), and King Obstinate (Sir Paul Richards) – all eventually knighted in Antigua and Barbuda for contributions to culture. There's no mentioning calypso royalty without a nod to Queen Ivena (Lena Phillip), the first woman to be crowned and whose first

performance in 2003 placed her among the stars.

While calypso continues to hold a special place, it has yielded some of its lure to the Party Monarch. This upstart competition is where young soca artistes thrive. For the contenders (among them, headliners Tian Winter, Ricardo Drue and Claudette "CP" Peters), music is not seasonal; it's their livelihoods, and it is they who now provide the jam tunes for the festival. This contest has grown from being outside the official calendar when it began in 1995 to attracting the largest crowds, with in excess of 12,000 patrons packing the Antigua Recreation Grounds made famous by cricket but transformed annually into 'Carnival City'. For action, go where the young and young at heart go: to the front of the stage. This is a show where crowd participation counts and is encouraged.

During Panorama, steel bands – some as large as 200-strong – battle for supremacy on the steel pan. The contest is a merging of

J'ouvert / JJ

Revellers from the 'Blue Devils' J'ouvert Troupe / JJ

young and old, veteran pannists and emerging players, male and female. Months practicing in the pan yard come down to eight minutes on stage. This competition predates Carnival with roots in 1949 and the Hell's Gate Steel Orchestra, which holds the distinction of being the world's oldest steel band and has the record for the most Panorama victories with eighteen titles.

Speaking of records, Colin Wanga Armstrong's Revellers Mas Troupe, with fourteen consecutive Band-of-the-Year titles, is revered on the road. But while history regards them fondly, on Carnival Monday and Tuesday the streets belong to no particular group but to the dancing and costumed mas' players en masse. It's a sight to behold.

J'ouvert, spanning the pre-dawn hours into late Monday morning, is when people dance in the streets to the music of the jam bands, steel bands and iron bands. There are numerous troupes these days, which appeal to those who favour uniformity. Others revel in jumping in and out of different bands, dashing through shortcuts across the close streets of the capital to catch up with friends.

Intertwined in the festival, which features several other shows, is the homecoming of thousands of transplanted Antiguans and Barbudans and the arrival of tourists. Integral to the festival are the roadside vendors who set up weeks in advance, selling everything from the latest fashions to bottled water.

Carnival is a time of egalitarian fervour. Tourists and locals jam together, politicians and the electorate shake their stuff, and captains of industry let loose alongside their staff. And as for the dancing style, 'wining' is part of the local DNA.

By first light on Wednesday morning, the streets are remarkably clean and people slip easily from costumes into work attire; it's enough to make some wonder if they imagined the spirited behaviour of the past few days. But that's the magic of Carnival and the sweet reprieve provides fuel for another year.

Mickel Brann-Challenger

Carnival Monday / JJ

The Blue Devils J'ouvert Troupe is the most popular troupe at Carnival / JJ

Panorama Competition / JJ

"Five decades of competitive sailing."

ANTIGUA SAILING WEEK

Antigua Sailing Week is one of the world's leading regattas, with over one hundred vessels from across the globe competing in five races that test endurance and skill. This spectacular event has grown over the years since a group of friends, sailors and hoteliers got together in the 1960s and organised a sailing event for boats from the USA, Canada and the Caribbean. It was given the name, 'Island for All Seasons' and was open to sailing boats, powerboats and fishing boats. Held in June, the organisers believed that the event would extend the country's tourism season. At its peak, over two hundred boats participated and although the types and sizes of boats have changed over the years, the emphasis is still on the racing, with the Guadeloupe to Antigua race a highly anticipated fixture. The date has changed to the last Sunday in April and first week of May and it has attracted bigger corporate sponsors and has become one of the Caribbean's leading attractions.

Almost five decades on, Antigua Sailing Week, which celebrates its Golden Jubilee in 2017, is a most popular annual fixture in the nation's calendar. For spectators, there are a number of viewing points from which to see everything from the mighty yachts to the smallest dinghies – from Shirley Heights to Carlisle Bay – as well as the opportunity to follow races on spectator boats.

What also makes Antigua Sailing Week an essential part of the local calendar is the numerous shore-side activities. These include opening parties, prize-giving ceremonies, concerts, and Lay Day which is held at Pigeon Point and is a day for the crews to unwind and participate in fun activities such as tug-o-war, a beach party as well as to watch the Nonsuch Bay RS Elite Challenge.

The event closes with Dockyard Day, where hundreds of residents join the sailing community at the historic Nelson's Dockyard for the official end of Antigua Sailing Week. It is a blend of cultural events, formal prize-giving, processions and the 'Beating of the Retreat' by the Royal Police Force of Antigua and Barbuda.

Brenda Lee Browne

Sailing across Morris Bay / JJ

Judging the participants of the Ministry of Tourism's annual Model Boat Race that takes place in Falmouth Harbour and precedes Antigua Sailing Week. The event, which marks its 20th anniversary in 2016, attracts many spectators and is a day for both the avid boat lover as well as the casual observer / JJ

Located on the English Harbour main road, Falmouth Harbour Marina has been specifically designed and built to cater for mega yachts. The facilities include wide, drive-on docks for easy access by VIP guests and for convenient provisioning; the supply of ultra-low sulphur diesel anywhere on the dock; electricity and water; garbage disposal and recycling; round the clock security; parking and a container park. All other facilities are within walking distance including shops, bars and a variety of restaurants nearby along with extensive marine services / Photo courtesy Ted Martin-Photo Fantasy Antigua

"21st century service from an eighteenth century dockyard."

NELSON'S DOCKYARD

Located in English Harbour, on the southern coast of Antigua, Nelson's Dockyard is the world's only working, Georgian-era dockyard. It was awarded World Heritage status by UNESCO in 2016 and is part of the Nelson's Dockyard National Park. The site is named after Britain's Admiral Horatio Nelson who, from 1784 to 1787, was Captain of the Leeward squadron of the Royal Navy stationed in Antigua.

Ruins of the officers' quarters at Shirley Heights / Photo Paul Zizka

Nelson's Dockyard is a busy hub both for sailing enthusiasts and tourists and is home to such world-renowned regattas as Antigua Sailing Week – the Caribbean's oldest regatta – and the Classic Yacht Regatta. It also offers a number of retail outlets and world-class marine services.

A significant feature of the dockyard is the historical architecture, including the sawpit shed (the oldest part of the existing facility, dating back to 1769); the sundial (made in 1777); the pillars (built in 1796); the naval officer's house (now a Museum); the stone wharf (originally built in 1821); and the ship's anchor (marking the spot where one officer shot another during a quarrel). All of these and more help transport visitors back to 18th and 19th century Antigua when the dockyard was a key part of the defence of Britain's interests in the Caribbean. It was from here that the seas were patrolled for ships violating the ban on the slave trade (illegal after 1807) or restrictions on trade with post-Independent America, in addition to guarding against attacks from rival European powers, particularly during the Napoleonic Wars. It was also the repair and maintenance centre for British ships operating in the Caribbean.

Shirley Heights Lookout is at the most southerly tip of Antigua. It is part of the Shirley Heights military complex and commands breathtaking views over English Harbour / Photo Boris Hudak

Although English Harbour has been in use since the 1600s, it was not until 1725 that buildings were erected in the dockyard to support the careening and repair of ships. In 1889, the dockyard was closed and later handed over to the local government in 1906. A group called the Friends of English Harbour Society spearheaded a programme of restoration beginning in 1951. The National Parks Authority now runs the day-to-day affairs of this historical gem.

Other fortifications, or former fortifications, in the park area include Fort Berkeley (built at the entrance to the dockyard in 1704), Shirley Heights (named after Governor Thomas Shirley who ordered the building of the fortifications around the dockyard for its protection in 1781), and Monk's Hill (initially built in 1689 as a refuge of last resort). Another historical building, Clarence House, overlooking the dockyard, has recently undergone significant restorations.

Notable attractions within the park area include the Pillars of Hercules (a spectacular, natural rock formation), the view from Shirley Heights Lookout (also the location of a longstanding Sunday fete), and the Copper and Lumber Store Hotel (a venue for another popular event, seafood Fridays).

Joanne C. Hillhouse

The remains of the original boat house and sail loft at Nelson's Dockyard. Built in 1797, visiting ships would tie up in the narrow central channel (wet dock) and the sails would be hoisted from the boats up to the sail loft through a trap door. Originally, the boat house was a large, two-storey building in which the ground floor was used for general storage and repairs, and the upper floor was used to repair and make sails. In 1845, the building was damaged by an earthquake, and in 1871, it was severely damaged by a hurricane. Today, all that remains of the original building are the boat house pillars, which have been capped with concrete to prevent water damage and further decay / Photo Frank Fell

Pillars Restaurant at The Admiral's Inn in Nelson's Dockyard / Photo Frank Fell

English Harbour is a natural harbour and settlement in the south of Antigua. The settlement takes its name from the nearby harbour in which Britain's Royal Navy established its base of operations for the area during the 18th century. English Harbour is a major centre of boating, especially yachting. There are two sheltered deepwater harbours – English Harbour itself and Falmouth Harbour / Photo Irishka777-Dreamstime

The Nelson's Dockyard Museum is housed on the ground floor of the original Naval Officer's House (Admiral's House) which dates back to 1855. On display are a number of items belonging to Britain's Admiral Horation Nelson, after whom the dockyard is named. Upstairs is dedicated to the military history of English Harbour. Nelson arrived in the Leeward Islands in 1784 as Captain of HMS Boreas and as head of a squadron of ships. His task was to enforce the shipping laws which prevented the trade of goods using foreign or American ships, and to develop the naval facilities in English Harbour / Photo Frank Fell

Heroes do not come along very often, but four men have earned this status in Antigua and Barbuda in a challenge that pitted them against the might of the Atlantic Ocean. The three Antiguans and one Briton, resident in Antigua for decades, successfully rowed from the Canary Islands to Antigua in the Talisker Whiskey Atlantic Challenge, dubbed 'the world's toughest row'. This remarkable feat earned them two entries in the *Guinness Book of World Records* – one for the oldest team of four to row cross the Atlantic and the other for the oldest rower (Peter Smith, 74) to cross the Atlantic.

The challenge, which took place from 20 December 2015 to 10 February 2016, also distinguishes them as not only the first Antiguan but also the first Caribbean team to take on this particular crossing.

"For years, I've been seeing them row across and come to Antigua," said team leader and instigator Dr Nicholas Fuller. "I didn't think there was any reason that we couldn't do it."

Fuller, J.D. Hall, Rowan "Archie" Bailey and Smith rowed 2600 nautical miles from La Gomera in the Canary Islands arriving at Nelson's Dockyard to a rousing reception from thousands of Antiguans who hailed them as heroes. It was a counter-point to the mocking laughter they received when they first announced their intentions to take up the challenge.

Their achievement has not only sparked a growing interest in rowing, it has also encouraged another team (Team Antigua) to begin preparations for the challenge in 2017. The experiences of Team Wadadli will be invaluable to the new participants - how to survive on limited resources; how to get along with others in a two-by-seven metre boat for 52 days; and how to prepare for an unexpected hurricane.

Members of the team cite their knowledge of the sea and of their vessel, patience, tolerance and a commitment to treating the challenge like a job, as key elements to their success.

The fame and hero status that came with the challenge was an obvious boon for the participants, but beyond the boat (named Wa'omani), the team also raised hundreds of thousands of dollars for the St John's Hospice.

Joanne C. Hillhouse

Arrival in Antigua / Photo courtesy of Antigua Atlantic Rowers

WORLD-CLASS MARINE ADMINISTRATION

The Department of Marine Services and Merchant Shipping (ADOMS) is the maritime administration of Antigua and Barbuda that offers a high quality ship and yacht registry and provides technical expertise to the broad national spectrum of ocean governance.

Established in 1986, the organisation is now ranked among the top registries in the world's merchant fleet. Ships and yachts flying the Antigua and Barbuda flag are welcome in all ports around the globe and are supported by a worldwide coverage of nautical professionals that perform statutory surveys, inspections, audits and issue mandatory statutory certificates that enable these vessels to trade.

As an archipelagic, twin-island state, Antigua and Barbuda is blessed with rights and responsibilities over an Exclusive Economic Zone (EEZ) of 107,914 sq km offering enormous potential for economic development and in marine transportation and logistics, fisheries, renewable energy and sustainable coastal and marine resource development.

ADOMS is committed to leveraging its operations, technical proficiency and international reputation to enhance confidence in the local yachting industry, attracting investments and boosting tourism. The completion of its new headquarters and multipurpose complex should greatly enhance the ability to optimise the vision of being a global purveyor of high quality maritime services that will potentially attract other components of the maritime cluster to Antigua and Barbuda.

Architectural design of the new headquarters and multipurpose complex / Image courtesy of ADOMS

"A walk on the wild side."

NATURAL WONDERS

Antigua and Barbuda is renowned for possessing some of the world's most impressive beaches, but there is so much more to be enjoyed.

A casual drive to the south of the island leads to Christian Valley where various trails offer different degrees of difficulty. The Valley boasts stunning views of fruit orchards, surrounding mountains, and quiet, tree-lined paths, perfect for the pensive wanderer. Bird-watching is popular in the Valley and visitors shouldn't be surprised to hear the shrill call of a gliding broad-winged hawk or feel unnerved when found under the careful scrutiny of an

The spectacular display of the frigate bird / Photo Schoolgirl-Dreamstime

American kestrel. The Valley is filled with regional endemic birds, rare and common, and from March to June, with migrants such as the brilliantly coloured American redstart. If visiting the valley after heavy showers of rain, a photograph at the Christian Valley Falls is a must.

On the north-western side of the island, McKinnon's Pond is a wetland perfect for viewing an abundance of sea and wetland birds. Its easy access allows the bird-watcher to observe the common gallinule and the threatened West Indian whistling duck. From early autumn to late spring, the quiet 'bird community' transforms into a bustling mix of both regional endemics and migrant birds: the attention-commanding osprey to the comedic gait of black-necked stilts to the ruddy turnstone, which travels thousands of miles to get to Antigua.

The offshore islands found in the North East Marine Management Area (NEMMA), a marine reserve, are of outstanding beauty and international biodiversity significance. This area, thanks to over two decades of conservation work by the Environmental Awareness Group and its partners, gives an appreciation of what Antigua and Barbuda was

Hiking trail near Fiennes Dam / JJ

Pond in Ebenezer / JJ

Green tree lizard / JJ

like before deforestation. There, free of foreign invasive species such as rats and mongooses, local wildlife thrives. On several, including Great Bird Island and Green Island, visitors may come across the world's once rarest snake, the harmless Antiguan racer and lizard species unique to these shores. This includes the brightly hued, portly Antiguan ground lizard. Also, many of the offshore islands are surrounded by several species of mangrove which provide a storm buffer to the mainland and provide a safe habitat for juvenile fish and birds.

During the nesting season from March to June, the NEMMA lights up with a spectacular show of birdlife: Magnificent frigate birds, hovering like kites, to red-billed tropicbirds with their long tail-feathers. Yellow warblers flit busily among the trees and mangrove cuckoos try to blend in with the branches on which they rest. A host of other birds – terns, herons, gulls,

hummingbirds and ducks – can be found on these islands.

Heading deeper into the marine world, both bottlenose and Atlantic spotted dolphins can be sighted all year long, while minke, pilot and humpback whales are mostly seen from February to May.

Sea turtles, once ubiquitous, are now all classified as endangered. Females of three species of sea turtle – green, hawksbill and leatherback – lumber up the beaches to nest on Antigua and Barbuda's shores. Occasionally, the loggerhead turtle can be seen foraging in waters around the islands.

With its rich ecosystem and biodiversity, the breaking of each new day presents a fresh opportunity to experience the wild side of Antigua and Barbuda.

Natalya Lawrence

A flurry of butterflies at Ffryes Beach / JJ

Seasonal waterfall in Christian Valley / JJ

Devil's Bridge is a natural rock arch on the rugged east coast of Antigua. The landscape around the 'bridge' features several natural blowholes which shoot up water and spray powered by waves from the **Atlantic Ocean** / Photo courtesy Antigua and Barbuda Tourism Authority

Body Pond / JJ

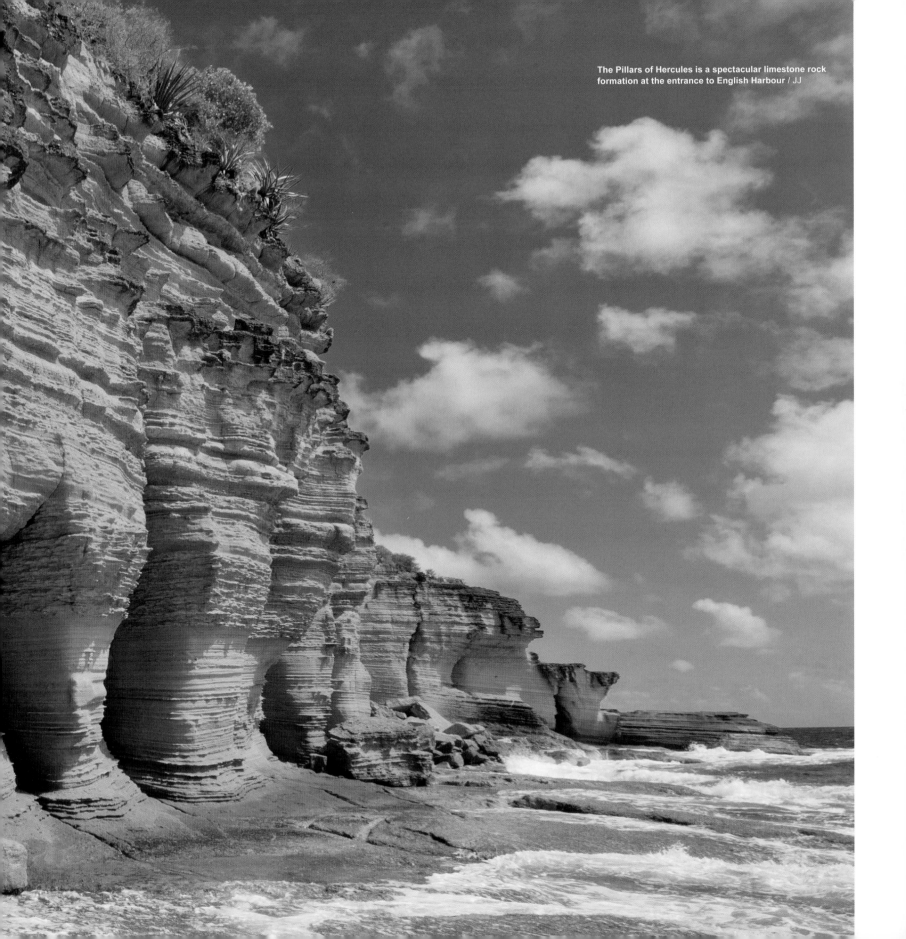

The Pillars of Hercules is a spectacular limestone rock formation at the entrance to English Harbour / JJ

"New life for beasts of burden."

A SAFE HAVEN FOR DONKEYS

For decades, the sight of donkeys carrying crops or people was a ubiquitous vision not just in Antigua and Barbuda but also throughout the Caribbean. Today, however, motorised alternatives have taken their place and some donkeys have been abandoned and are roaming free.

To combat this sometimes hazardous occurrence, the Antigua Donkey Sanctuary takes in and cares for these former 'beasts of burden'.

Established in 1993, and located near Bethesda in the parish of St Phillip's, the facility is managed by the Antigua and Barbuda Humane Society.

With more than 150 donkeys in its care, the sanctuary offers a peaceful environment that is also open to the public. Entrance is free and visitors have an opportunity to feed and pet these adorable creatures. The sanctuary is funded by donations from compassionate benefactors as well as through its 'adopt a donkey' scheme, where participants pay a small annual fee towards their chosen animal's care.

Brenda Lee Browne

"Fans are knowledgeable and passionate."

SPORT IN ANTIGUA AND BARBUDA

For several decades the most famous sporting facility in Antigua and Barbuda was the Antigua Recreation Grounds (ARG), home to some spectacular cricket events. World records were set and smashed, and fans across the globe danced to the tunes played by the only non-cricketing 'Man of the Match', DJ Chickie. It was party and cricket – the trademark of international cricket matches in Antigua from the late 1970s to the late 1990s.

The ARG was as famous as the cricketers who travelled from the local and regional cricket scene to forge international careers that have placed them in the annals of cricket history – Sir Vivian Richards, Sir Andy Roberts, Sir Curtly Ambrose and Sir Richie Richardson all hail from this twin-island nation.

The ICC Cricket World Cup, held in 2007 in the Caribbean, saw the building of a new ground – the Sir Vivian Richards Cricket Grounds, now renamed as the Sir Vivian Richards Stadium – located on the Sir Sydney Walling Highway. Antiguan and Barbudan Sir Sydney Walling is often regarded as one of the greatest batsmen from the Eastern Caribbean to not play for the West Indies.

Although the stadium has been adapted to host major national events including the annual Youth Rally, National Awards Ceremony and Food Fair held during the country's Independence celebrations, it serves as the home for local and international cricket in Antigua and Barbuda.

The West Indies Cricket Board (WICB), the governing body of cricket across the Caribbean, also has its headquarters in Antigua on the outskirts of the capital, St John's. Plans are afoot for the WICB to move its operations to a new facility complete with a practice ground and gymnasium.

However, there is more to the Antigua and Barbuda sports scene than just cricket. Basketball, cycling, football, golf, volleyball, netball, tennis, horse racing, deep sea fishing, sailing, kitesurfing, swimming and, more recently, triathlon and drag racing, have gained popularity, with facilities being upgraded and built to meet the demands of participants and spectators.

A number of student athletes, meanwhile, have gained scholarships to US colleges and UK universities across different sporting disciplines.

The sporting calendar runs throughout the year and events are open to the public. The atmosphere on these occasions is often vibrant,

'Gravy', as he is known locally, was a regular feature at cricket matches in Antigua. Along with Chickie's Hi-Fi, he transformed the way cricket was supported and enjoyed by fans in Antigua and Barbuda / JJ

Football practice at Trinity Academy / JJ

Horse racing at Cassada Gardens Turf Club / JJ

as fans are both knowledgeable and passionate; and music and food always add to the spectacle.

In recent years, the success of the national football team has resulted in international matches featuring teams from South America and the US being held at the Sir Vivian Richards Stadium.

Sports clubs, academies and youth programmes take place both during the school term and at summer camps – some facilitated by past international players such as Kenny Benjamin and Winston Benjamin. The temperate winter and spring climate attracts teams, both youth as well as senior, from the UK to come and practice, working with coaches and clubs across the island thus expanding the country's sports tourism mandate.

Golfers may, on any given day, find themselves playing a round with cricket legends Sir Vivian Richards and Sir Richie Richardson, both avid golfers who play tournaments at home and across the region.

While for the armchair athletes, local cable television stations and sports bars have ample coverage of international leagues and championships.

Brenda Lee Browne

Sunday morning basketball at the King
George V Grounds in Gray's Farm / JJ

Bikers on the nature trail near Body Pond / JJ

Drag racing at the North Sound International Raceway / JJ

Antigua and Barbuda Sport Fishing Tournament / JJ

Bimini start of the Antigua and Barbuda Sport Fishing Tournament / JJ

Kitesurfing in Antigua has grown in popularity / Photo Fotoswiat-Dreamstime

St John's Cathedral in the nation's capital is also known as St John the Divine, and the Cathedral Church of the Diocese of North Eastern Caribbean and Aruba, and it is an Anglican church / JJ

"A cornerstone of life in paradise."

RELIGION

Antigua and Barbuda is a predominantly Christian nation. Images of the Anglican Cathedral of Saint John the Divine, also known locally as "big church", adorn tourist postcards. It has historical appeal; its present structure, seated atop Newgate Street in St John's since the 1800s, is a location the Anglicans have claimed since the 1600s. Meanwhile, at Parham village is the Georgian masterpiece that is St

Peter's Anglican Church, with its irregular octagonal shape and boat-hull-like wooden ceiling. These are only two of the many historical churches on island.

The latest census (2011) registers around 76 per cent of Antigua and Barbuda's almost 85,000 strong population as Christian. The Anglican Church, present since 1634, accounts for around 17 per cent of the population. Later arrivals, in the form of the Adventist and Pentecostal Churches, follow with around 12 per cent each. The Methodist, Roman Catholic, Baptist, Moravian, Church of God and Weslyan Holiness Churches account for less than 10 per cent of the population. Other religious groups claim around 12 per cent of the population and include the Rastafarians, Hindus, Baha'is, Muslims and Jews.

The nation's churches embody a strong tradition of outreach. The Moravian and Methodists began as ministries to the enslaved Africans. In fact, Antigua is considered the 'cradle of Methodism' in the Caribbean, which has been here since 1760; and the Female Refugee Society, considered to be the first benevolent society in Antigua, was established in 1817 by local Wesleyan Methodists. Meanwhile, the Anglican Reverend Robert

St Peter's Anglican Church in Parham dates back to the mid-1800s / JJ

The renovated Ebenezer Methodist Church / JJ

St Philip's Anglican Church in St Philip was built in the early nineteenth century / JJ

Newfield Enon Moravian Church / JJ

Methodist Church in Freetown / JJ

Holberton, appointed as the St John's Rector in 1827, was so renowned for his attention to the ailing and suffering that the island's previous main hospital was named after him. The churches' tradition of assistance continues today via many noteworthy efforts such as the Sunshine Home for Girls, opened in 1992 by the Salvation Army (established in Antigua in 1903) and the interdenominational Antigua Street Pastors programme (established in 2006).

The nation's churches have also played a significant role in the field of education. In 1813, the Methodists opened the first schoolroom in Antigua, and perhaps the West Indies, for enslaved Africans. The Moravians (present since 1756) are often heralded for their earlier training of many schoolmasters and mistresses who went on to serve in institutions throughout the Caribbean. Today, private schools operated by churches (Catholic, Lutheran, Baptist and others) are held in high esteem.

Rastafarians, through their influence on music, hair, dress, speech and 'ital food'; the contributions of the Salvation Army Band; the Moravian and Anglican food fairs; and the Catholic Church's Vitus Mas troupe's past participation in the nation's annual Carnival, are further examples of the ways religious groups add to the culture.

Dr Hazra C. Medica

"An alternative way of life."

RASTAFARI IN ANTIGUA AND BARBUDA

The Rastafari movement first appeared in Antigua and Barbuda in the late 1960s. Early followers rejected materialism and chose to live a natural way of life and a withdrawal from mainstream society. The wearing of 'dreadlocks' and consuming a vegetarian (i-tal) diet are also features of Rastafari.

By the early 1970s, communities were established in Cooks, an area on the outskirts of St John's, and dubbed 'the Jungle', and the 'One Love' community in Bendals, among others.

These communities were met with resentment by the general public and the authorities. Many brethren (followers of Rastafari) suffered harassment and were even arrested for such offences as 'wandering abroad' and being 'of no fixed place of abode'. The settlements were also subject to acts of vandalism and physical assaults. Another type of assault concerned the 'shearing' of locks of imprisoned Rastafari and the banning of dreadlocks in schools. However, in 1992, an historic Government decision outlawed these practices. Furthermore, in 1996, a constitutional redress motion in the High Court received judicial acknowledgment that Rastafari is a religion entitled to constitutional protection.

The movement was further consolidated by visits from prominent Rastafari delegations from Jamaica, the birthplace of the Rastafari movement. The Rastafari Nyabinghi Theocracy (the spiritual essence of the Rastafari tradition) was established and other sections within the movement were established, most notably, the Ethiopian African Black International Congress, known as the Bobo Shanti.

Antigua and Barbuda is a founding member of the Caribbean Rastafari Organisation (CRO), established in 1998. The CRO is a member of the CARICOM NGO grouping Caribbean Policy Development Centre and the Caribbean Pan African Network, and has held discussions with the African Union and participated in AU/CARICOM meetings.

Over the years there has been growing acceptance and understanding of Rastafari principles and way of life, including the use of marijuana (hola herb) for medicinal and sacramental purposes.

The year 2016 marks the 50th anniversary of the visit to Jamaica by Ethiopia's Emperor Haile Selassie I, who is revered as the Messiah by the Rastafari faith.

Ras Franki/Franklin Francis

African Liberation Day being comemorated by members of the Rastafari community at the Prince Klass Memorial / JJ

"A feast of culinary delights."

A PARADISE FOR FOOD-LOVERS

Antigua and Barbuda is a food-lovers' paradise, whether its street food, home-cooked recipes or restaurants serving the finest Caribbean and international cuisine.

The weekend is when many put away their pots and pans and head to their favourite eating spot for johnnie cakes (fried dough balls), roast corn, salt fish fritters, goat or conch water (a spicy, hot broth served in cups), fried fish, souse (a sauce made with pickled meats), barbecue chicken, burgers, ribs, seasoned rice, rice pudding (similar to blood pudding, with rice) or jerk chicken. And many of these delights are available from roadside vendors. Among the array of vegetarian options, there is ital (or i-tal)

cuisine, which are vegan dishes that are the staple of followers of the Rastafari faith.

The arrival of people of Arabic, Chinese and Indian heritage, and a mix of nationals from other parts of the Caribbean, including the French and Spanish Caribbean, has added shawarma, falafel, stir-fried dishes, doubles, roti, dhal, butter chicken and more to the national menu.

Food is an essential ingredient at most occasions in Antigua and Barbuda, from sports and community events, to church fairs and shows. Barbecue pits, made from oil drums and coal pots (locally made red clay or iron cooking stands) are all familiar sights.

For the 'seated' dining experience, there are many restaurants offering everything from pizzas and burgers to haute cuisine. Most hotels have their own restaurants and bars but there are a number of other food outlets across the nation that offer a wide variety of specialist menus. These include seafood, French, Italian, Sushi, Asian fusion and Caribbean dishes.

Among the many offerings are the national/ traditional dishes including pepper pot (a green vegetable-based dish with root vegetables, chicken, salt beef/pork and dumplings), fungee (a cornmeal dish much like polenta), salt fish,

choba (aubergines) and chop-up (greens and spinach). During the Easter period, Antiguans and Barbudans spend hours grating sweet potatoes and coconut, before combining both with flour and water to create ducana – a large dumpling traditionally wrapped in sea grape or banana leaves and boiled.

Barbuda is known for its abundance of seafood and menus on Antigua's sister island include lobster and a wide variety of fish. Rice, peas and mutton-based dishes are also popular.

The twin-island nation is also well-known for its fruit, from, in particular, the Antigua black pineapple to mangoes (the main feature of the annual Mango Festival), sugar apples, bananas, guineps, sour sops, avocados, citrus fruits, golden apples, cherries and tamarinds – all sold in the public market in St John's and from many roadside vendors.

Visitors to Antigua and Barbuda are encouraged to sample the many culinary delights on offer and, before leaving, to purchase a Caribbean cookbook, some black cake and a bottle of rum as reminders of their journey to a little bit of paradise.

Brenda Lee Browne

OJ's Beach Bar & Restaurant / JJ

"Rum is not merely a drink, it's a tradition."

RAISING THE SPIRITS

"Rum! Rum! Rum!" intoned Kenne Blessin in his 2011 soca hit, 'Spirit is in my Cup'. Not that it was the first song in tribute to the art of libation but something about that mellow tune brings to mind a comfortable seat on a porch facing west at sunset, and a glass of coconut water with a good shot of English Harbour rum.

Conversely, Ricardo Drue's 'Professional Drinker' conjures up a swarm of bodies, sweatin' and fetin', with drinks – whether Cavalier and coke, or Koko Karibe and pineapple juice, or a stiff Cavalier Rum Punch – held aloft.

Rum in Antigua and Barbuda is not merely a drink, it's a tradition. In a reference to the days of slavery and colonialism, calypso King Obstinate sang, "From black hands, sweet sugar flowed" – but just as important to the English economy was that *other* by-product of the cane fields: rum. And it was on this liquid industry (since 1674) that many solid fortunes were made and bequeathed to this day. Just as, on the other side of the counter, many more fortunes and inheritances were unmade.

Rum flowed downhill, and from being the British planter's preference to tea, the drink became favoured by all classes and races. Today, local production is largely for local consumption – from lawyer to labourer, politician to priest; at the trendy bar, the countryside rum shop, the Carnival fete, the cricket match and the domino table.

No matter the array of beverages, no self-respecting host or hostess would consider the bar complete without several choices of white and dark rum. No christening, or wedding, or funeral repast is a success without it. Hold the fruits if you like, but be sure to pour a bottle into that Christmas cake. And no flag-waving Antiguan or Barbudan living abroad would dare return to North America or the UK without a "Cavi" for the other waiting patriots, thirsty for a sip of home.

Young fellows graduate to manhood when they learn to hold their liquor, moving seamlessly from "nice" to "sarl" to "tone sarl" with nary a stagger and hardly a slur. Some learn to hold their juice so well – or "to powder" – they earn the distinction of being called "Rum Dawg". Others are "called to the bar" and never leave. And while you will seldom see locals holding a cigarette, you will always see them toting a shot glass.

So our visitors now know the correct response to, "What you drinking?" It's always, "Rum."

D. Gisele Isaac

196

Local bar in Willikies, eastern Antigua / JJ

"Home-based food producers are now household names."

AGRICULTURE

It was not so long ago that cane fields were a familiar site across Antigua and although serious sugar cane production has all but disappeared from the national economy, agriculture makes up four per cent of the national GDP. Smallholdings, individual farmers, backyard farmers and school agricultural projects are still producing vegetables, fruits, sugar cane, coconut water, poultry and eggs.

The country's main market is in the capital, St John's, and it is a lively venue especially on Saturdays. Street vendors also ply their trade along the major highways.

Local products from
Granma Aki / JJ

An increased awareness of where food is sourced has seen a rise in organically produced food. Agro-processing is also on the increase and, in many cases, these producers established their businesses at home. Products include jams and preserves, pepper sauces, tea (referred to locally as 'bush tea' and used for generations as a cure-all), food snacks such as dried fruit, coconut and banana chips, soaps (using natural oils and goats' milk) and pure coconut oil which is used for hair and body lotions as well as for cooking. A number of these once small, home-based industries have now become household names, such as Susie's Hot Sauce, Raw Island Products and Granma Aki.

The increased interest in local food production has resulted in a number of popular events built around the industry. Established in 2005, the Antigua and Barbuda Mango Festival takes place in the summer when the fruit is plentiful, and the Urlings Fisheries Complex in the south of Antigua hosts seasonal seafood festivals.

Antigua and Barbuda is not immune to the ravages of over-fishing and pollution and, therefore, robust fishing restrictions have been implemented. While marine fish, lobster, conch, cockle, etc are available in season,

The Antigua black pineapple / J.L.

Rosey Macmaster of Suzie's Hot Sauce is one of Antigua's most successful local producers / JJ

supermarkets, hotels and restaurants are not allowed to sell or serve these items out of season. Initiatives like the Blue Halo Project in Barbuda (a project of the WAITT Institute in the US and partner governments) has drafted a plan for coastal sanctuaries to encourage the replenishment and sustainable use of the marine resources surrounding the sister island.

Traditional animal husbandry is still practiced. Goat, sheep, pig and cattle farmers are still seen across the island. The meat is sold at the meat market in downtown St John's and in supermarkets. Domestic poultry and egg production also serves the local markets.

The Antigua and Barbuda government recognises the importance of the local agricultural sector and has pledged increased monetary assistance to the national Central Marketing Corporation (CMC) – an agency created in 1979 through the Ministry of Agriculture to help improve the production and marketing of local products. Today, CMC sells farm and agro-processed products through its outlet, adjacent to the Public Market, while encouraging people to buy local and supporting local production to feed the nation and for export.

Of all the produce grown in Antigua and Barbuda, the most famous is the Antigua black pineapple, a small and incredibly sweet fruit grown in the south of the island.

Fruit, vegetables and ground provisions
at St John's Market / JJ

Breadfruit is a species of flowering tree that originated in the South Pacific. British and French navigators introduced a few seedless varieties to the Caribbean islands during the late 18th century. Its name is derived from the texture of the moderately ripe fruit when cooked, similar to freshly baked bread / JJ

St John's Public Fish Market, wharf and the catch of the day / JJ

Heritage Quay / JJ

"From souvenirs to savoury delights."

SHOPPING IN PARADISE

Shopping while travelling, as well as acquiring any number of typical souvenirs, is all about taking home the spirit and energy of the destination – a keepsake to transport you back to the place or special moment during your stay.

It is essential, therefore, that any traveller should spend time in Antigua and Barbuda's capital, St John's. It is here that the two main shopping areas are located: Heritage Quay and Redcliffe Quay. Both have a wide selection of delights on offer, but each one offers a distinctly different experience.

Heritage Quay was built in the late 1980s and is the main docking port of entry for cruise visitors. On 'cruise ship days', it is a hive of activity. Between the ground and upper levels, shoppers can find world-class international brands in clothes, jewellery, handbags, eyewear and more.

A short walk away is Redcliffe Quay with its quaint shops that are ideal for the shopper who is interested in a more cultural experience. The old red brick buildings were built in the late nineteenth and early twentieth centuries and are now home to dozens of intriguing shops.

There are also a number of enchanting dining options that allow the traveller to savour the delights of Antiguan and Barbudan cuisine.

Michelle George

Vendor's kiosk at Turner's Beach / JJ

"Hundreds of locations for the perfect Caribbean wedding."

GETTING MARRIED IN ANTIGUA AND BARBUDA

Antigua and Barbuda is the perfect destination for couples to tie the knot; and with 365 beaches, there are literally hundreds of locations for the perfect Caribbean wedding.

Whatever the theme, local wedding co-ordinators can make it happen. For that special occasion, choices range from an intimate ceremony to the most elaborate event - and always with the enchanting Caribbean as the

backdrop. The natural environment and the joy of the occasion combine to work their magic: white-sand beach, white linen, orchids, bougainvillea leaves, the gentle surf of the Caribbean Sea and the soothing rhythms of a steel pan - what could be better?

The wedding breakfast can take place on the beach, in a hotel or at a restaurant with almost any type of cuisine available – from the exquisite local dishes to the finest international fare.

Honeymoon options include secluded hotels and villas - from the most luxurious to the smaller boutique hotels.

For the adventurous, there are helicopter tours, off-road buggies, snorkelling, windsurfing on the Atlantic side of the island, hikes to Rendezvous Bay, Orange Valley, or along any of the country's beautiful trails, and day-trips to the islets around Antigua and Barbuda.

These are just some of the treats on offer for those who choose to get married in a little bit of paradise.

Couples are advised to check the calendar to see what's happening and then just leave it to the local wedding planner to organise the perfect Caribbean wedding and honeymoon.

Zahra I. Airall

"Antigua and Barbuda is open for business."

BUSINESS GROWTH AND DEVELOPMENT IN PARADISE

Antigua and Barbuda has been referred to as 'a little bit of paradise' since the mid-1940s. Back then, a group of wealthy Americans had identified Antigua as the perfect Caribbean location for establishing the Mill Reef Club - a private resort aimed at other wealthy individuals who could come and enjoy the delights of Antigua.

Today, Antigua and Barbuda is characterised by a service-based economy, with tourism and government services representing the largest sources of employment and income. Tourism and tourism-related economic activities, including sectors such as construction, financial services, transportation and real estate, account for over two-thirds of gross domestic product (GDP).

The Gaston Browne Administration that took the leadership of Government in 2014, has aggressively pursued the recovery and growth of the economy, and focused attention on implementing structural transformation, attracting foreign direct investment, reviving the private sector and encouraging public-private sector development. Prime Minister Browne has issued the challenge to embrace the economic vision to develop Antigua and Barbuda into an "economic powerhouse of the Caribbean", and advocated a path of 'entrepreneurial socialism foundation' to stabilise the economy, increase lifestyle benefits and employment, and prepare the country for dramatic growth.

A prime example of public-private partnership was demonstrated in 2015 when the Government purchased 100 per cent ownership of the West Indies Oil Company (WIOC), a corporation that held the exclusive importation of all fuel supplies into the country. WIOC was previously controlled by a European investor but the Government arranged local bank financing for the purchase and was subsequently able to recover the cost by selling 49 per cent of the shares to business entities, covering the entire cost of its purchase price and allowing the Government to separate certain lands that were acquired in the original purchase. The acquisition has caused a multiplier effect in the economy. In 2016, the Government established another public-private partnership by purchasing almost 80 per cent of the voting stock of the indigenous financial institution, Caribbean Union Bank, thereby strengthening the stability of the financial sector and enabling the bank to competitively enhance its services and products for clients and to support the general economy.

The economic environment is being supported by significant improvements to the

St John's Harbour / Photo
Sergey Kelin

national infrastructure across all key sectors: the new international airport terminal - which is attracting more carriers and visitors to Antigua and Barbuda; the modernisation of the St John's Deep Water Harbour as a commercial trans-shipment centre and a tourist hub for major cruise lines; a comprehensive road programme; additional reverse osmosis water plants to ensure adequate delivery to consumers; an investment in green energy, with a 10 MWp solar farm facility and 2,000 solar street lights; improved broadband and e-Government services; a substantially enhanced healthcare system; and upgraded public education facilities.

Domestic and international financial services continue to meet international standards and the jurisdiction is considered compliant with the requirements of international authorities, including the Financial Action Task Force (FATF), the Organisation for Economic Co-operation and Development (OECD) and its Common Reporting Standards, and the US Foreign Account Tax Compliance Act (FATCA). As a stable, democratic and sovereign country, blessed with some of the world's most attractive real estate, Antigua and Barbuda is a well-regarded destination for foreign direct investment and international business. It is able to offer international economic zones and financial services to meet the challenges and requirements of a connected financial world. Its attraction is further enhanced by the growing performance of the Citizenship by Investment Program (CIP) which earns substantial non-tax revenue. These earnings are used by Government to support a variety of fiscal measures that have helped to reduce the national debt, meet certain salaries and wages, and ensure a cleaner nation.

Antigua and Barbuda is appropriately reorganising itself to meet the requirements of modern business and the surge of global demands for investment solutions to serve international business, wealth management and financial services. The combination of a modern infrastructure with well-regulated financial service providers and the ability to evaluate attractive investment opportunities, including the benefit to qualify for citizenship, makes Antigua and Barbuda a preferred location for doing business.

Brian Stuart-Young

"Economic co-operation with generous grant funding."

CHINA RELATIONS BLOSSOM

Within two years of Antigua and Barbuda becoming an independent nation in 1981, the then Prime Minister, V.C. Bird, established diplomatic relations with the People's Republic of China and led a delegation to Beijing in 1983. Prime Minister Bird became the first leader in the Eastern Caribbean to extend friendship and co-operation with China, whom he termed as the "sleeping giant" that would wake and influence the world. Over the subsequent years, Antigua and Barbuda's relationship with China continued to grow strongly, and it was not surprising that within two months of the current Prime Minister, Gaston Browne, taking control of the Government, he too led a state visit to Beijing in 2014 to exchange diplomatic greetings with President Xi Jinping and Premier Li Keqiang. The Gaston Browne Administration appointed professional Antiguan banker, Brian Stuart-Young as its Non-Resident Ambassador to China.

Over more than thirty years, the relationship of friendly co-operation between the two nations has blossomed and borne much fruit, and today Antigua and Barbuda recognises China as a key relationship. The bilateral and high-level exchanges are frequent; the political respect and mutual trust continues to grow; the areas of pragmatic co-operation consistently expand; the people to people and culture exchanges are increasing; and China and Antigua and Barbuda support and co-ordinate closely with each other on international affairs. The Government gifted the Government of China with five acres of prime residential land in 2016 to facilitate the construction of a permanent embassy and office complex.

The economic co-operation extended by China includes generous grant funding that facilitated several important projects including the construction of the Sir Vivian Richards Cricket Stadium and the Five Islands Educational Institution. Current funding also includes the development of the Grays Green Community Centre and Indoor Basketball Court as well as two other planned community centres with polyclinics in St John's City West and St Phillips North locations; agricultural and housing projects; and annual support to the Defence and Police Forces. In education and cultural development, twenty new scholarships are granted to local students to attend senior Chinese universities each year, and Antigua will host a Confucius Institute to expand language and cultural development.

Significant support through concessional funding from China's Export-Import Bank was

also obtained and used for major infrastructure projects including an electricity power plant and, more recently, the construction of a new international airport terminal, which is considered amongst the best airport hubs in the region and has the potential to process 2000 people per hour. The modern terminal has attracted several new airlines and increased the seat capacity to Antigua and Barbuda. Passenger convenience is enhanced with the introduction of four jet bridges, multiple VIP lounges and expanded duty-free shopping.

China is supporting a complimentary infrastructure project for the modernisation of the St John's Deepwater Harbour Port. The technical design, completed by the Chinese firm China Civil Engineering Construction Corporation, who were also contracted for the airport terminal, will significantly upgrade the existing port that is now over fifty years old and could not accommodate the growth of commerce projected for the economy. The modernisation programme will enable the port to be a convenient trans-shipment hub for improving container cargo services and also to expand cruise ship accommodation for tourism services. The operation of these China-facilitated activities would make Antigua the crossroads for commercial shipping across the Caribbean and support the Government's cohesive master plan to double the number of annual cruise ship visitors and establish the market of homeport cruise visitors.

The Government established visa-free entry for the Chinese and efforts are progressing to leverage the strong friendship and co-operation with China to arrange convenient air communications to Antigua, which will be attractive to encourage Chinese tourists and allow Antigua to be the gateway for Chinese visitors to the Caribbean.

Built to replace its ageing terminal, the new, state-of-the-art facility at V.C. Bird International Airport became operational in August 2015. It is the largest airport in the Leeward Islands and now handles nearly one million passengers each year. It boasts four jet bridges, modern passenger processing and security screening and five baggage carousels among its many state-of-the-art features / JJ

The new terminal at V.C. Bird International Airport has forty-six check-in desks and fifteen self-check kiosks / JJ

Opened in 2015, the new terminal at V.C. Bird International Airport offers a wider selection of amenities than previously available including a mini food court, more retail outlets and VIP and first class lounges / JJ

"A transition from old to new."

HOUSING

Traditional housing in Antigua and Barbuda suffered a major blow in 1950 when many of the residences were destroyed or severely damaged by two hurricanes. Making land-fall within ten days of each other, hurricanes Baker and Dog left 12,000 people homeless.

Prompted by the Antigua Trades and Labour Union, the government implemented a programme of building low-cost housing. Instead of constructing the houses out of timber, or wattle and daub, they were built using cement blocks and galvanised metal. A number of developments were established to cater for the influx of people who were, at the time, leaving the sugar estates.

In 1974, Antigua and Barbuda suffered an earthquake, and in 1995, the twin-island nation was hit by hurricane Luis – the most costly and destructive disaster in the country's history. However, the hurricanes of 1950 will be noted for the way in which they transformed the housing sector.

As Antigua and Barbuda continues to modernise, its housing stock will reflect the transition from old to new and, in many cases, while standing side-by-side. Nowhere is this more evident than in the capital, St John's. Here, colonial architecture and historic buildings rub shoulders with ultra-modern edifices and glazed facades.

A modern Antiguan home / Photo Linda Johnsonbaugh

Urlings village / JJ

The Antigua and Barbuda Defence Force (ABDF) was established in 1981, the same year that the nation achieved its Independence from Great Britain. Over its three and half decades, the force has evolved from an organisation that catered solely for the defence of the nation's territorial integrity and a support to law enforcement, to an institution that now provides greater support to the civil authority, as well as a facilitator in the area of national and regional development.

Among its many responsibilities, the ABDF, through its 1st Antigua and Barbuda Regiment, provides security at key government installations, assistance to the police force in its crime-fighting operations, and the tactical training of its personnel to make them combat ready for any conflict within the region.

In 1995, the Antigua and Barbuda Police Marine Unit was transferred to the ABDF and renamed the ABDF Coast Guard. The service provides a number of naval operations including marine law enforcement, fisheries protection, drug interdiction, prevention of smuggling (human trafficking and goods) and oil pollution response.

The ABDF also commands the Antigua and Barbuda National Cadet Corps. First established in 1966 at the Antigua Grammar School, the corps was expanded in 2004 to include a sea unit.

The Antigua and Barbuda Defence Force has now developed into an effective and comprehensive service capable of dealing with natural and human disasters as well as all manner of emergencies at home and across the region.

Major Telbert Benjamin

1st Antigua and Barbuda Regiment / Photo ABDF

228

TAKING THE PROFIT OUT OF CRIME

The Office of National Drug and Money Laundering Control Policy (ONDCP) is a law enforcement agency charged with responsibilities to combat drug trafficking, money laundering and terrorism financing.

From its establishment in 1996, the ONDCP has worked vigorously to achieve its mandate. In the battle against drug trafficking, the organisation has been achieving increasing successes in the interdiction of illegal drugs and stemming the trans-shipment of drugs through Antigua and Barbuda.

The ONDCP also supervises financial institutions with continuous examinations and support to ensure that they have effective systems to deter, detect and report the proceeds of crime and terrorism financing.

Though a comparatively small law enforcement agency, the organisation has excelled in its performance having attained a number of significant achievements. These include obtaining the first civil forfeiture order, which was made against property of a drug trafficker. Further, the organisation was able to record the first confiscation in Antigua and Barbuda under the Proceeds of Crime Act. In 2016, the ONDCP successfully enforced the forfeiture of US $66.7 million that were the proceeds of corruption in a foreign country. By these and other successes, the agency continues to distinguish itself while living up to its motto, "Taking the profit out of crime".

Over the years, the ONDCP has maintained its vigilance by working with the legislative arm of government to ensure that appropriate laws and regulations are enacted and enforced in maintaining international standards. Equipped with a staff of qualified, highly trained and committed individuals, the organisation continues to play its role in making Antigua and Barbuda one of the safest tourist destinations in the world with an aim to become the leading Caribbean law enforcement agency combating, drug trafficking, money laundering and terrorism financing.

ONDCP Headquarters /
Photo ONDCP

The reservoir at Potworks Dam is reputed to be the largest
expanse of freshwater in the Eastern Caribbean / JJ

ANTIGUA AND BARBUDA IS GOING GREEN

On approach to the VC Bird International airport, passengers may notice a field of black panels amid Antigua's beautiful landscape of green hills and colourful houses. The panels are part of Antigua and Barbuda's biggest solar farm and are the linchpin in the country's renewable energy program. Commissioned in 2005, the solar farm produces an estimated three megawatts of electricity that provides most of the energy for the airport. It is estimated that within six months of being installed, the solar farm not only exceeded the expected amount of electricity generation, but also reduced local CO_2 emissions by 2,000 tons, representing a significant reduction in the nation's carbon footprint.

However, the solar farm is just the first step in a plan to install ten megawatts of clean energy in Antigua and Barbuda.

Close by lies another critical piece in the country's green puzzle: the Antigua and Barbuda Waste Recycling Corporation. This non-profit organisation, in partnership with a number of government agencies, collects recyclable items either for processing and local reuse or for export.

It also conducts significant outreach initiatives to educate and inform the public around the greening mission, including an interschool recycling competition in which over 55 schools compete for prizes while cleaning up the country.

The government has also implemented a ban on small plastic grocery bags. Plastic waste is a major environmental problem - from clogging up drains and waterways, to harming marine life - and Antigua and Barbuda is one of the first Caribbean countries to completely ban these products.

The efforts to push a cleaner and greener Antigua and Barbuda are taking root. These include a reduction in the taxes for electric vehicles, and the birth of environmentally-friendly companies like Themba Biofuels which takes used vegetable oil to create bio diesel, a biodegradable and non-toxic alternative to diesel.

With the global threat of climate change, Antigua and Barbuda is playing its part in ensuring that the green movement is well under way.

Daryl George

A VALUABLE SOURCE OF FRESH WATER

The reservoir at Potworks Dam is reputed to be the largest expanse of freshwater in the Eastern Caribbean. It is about a mile long and half a mile wide and, when full, can hold around one billion gallons of water. The water is retained by two dams - the Potworks dam at the eastern end and the Delaps dam at the south.

The site is named after an 18th century pottery works that was located at the Garden estate, and which was owned by the Codrington family from the early 18th to the end of the 20th century. Skilled potters produced mainly conical sugar pots that were used for draining molasses from raw sugar.

Potworks Dam was planned in the late 1960s and was officially opened in 1970. It is meant to augment the country's fresh water supply which suffers from a severe lack of rainfall.

ANTIGUA AND BARBUDA IS A MEDICAL NEXUS

Antigua and Barbuda's position within the Eastern Caribbean makes it an ideal location from which to provide leading medical services throughout the region.

The past two decades have seen the development of advanced medical facilities and training from overseas, and the country now has the capability to serve as the final referral centre for tertiary medical care.

The country's main public hospital is Mount St John's Medical Centre located in the capital. It offers all the services expected of a modern hospital, including an advanced surgical facility and a network of satellite clinics. Surgical procedures are also available at two, state-of-the-art private clinics. A number of clinics also provide specialist services in areas such as obstetrics and gynaecology.

Antigua and Barbuda provides extensive medical services to residents, tourists and visitors, as well as to referred patients from across the Caribbean.

Dr K.K. Singh

THE AMERICAN UNIVERSITY OF ANTIGUA COLLEGE OF MEDICINE

The American University of Antigua (AUA) College of Medicine is an innovative medical school dedicated to providing education of the highest quality, granting opportunities to under-represented minorities, fostering a diverse academic community and ensuring that its graduates develop the skills and attitudes of lifelong learning, compassion and professionalism.

The university was founded with the commitment to support under-served communities and address the impending physician shortage with an emphasis on primary care. As such, it recognises its social responsibility to advance the field of medicine and lead the next generation of physicians and healthcare professionals to respond to global healthcare needs.

In just over ten years, AUA has surpassed significant milestones and earned essential accreditations, making it one of the top medical schools in the Caribbean, with graduates practicing throughout the United States, United Kingdom and Canada. This success is due, in large part, to the nation of Antigua and Barbuda which has enriched the AUA community and become a welcome home to the institution and its students.

ADVOCACY IN ANTIGUA AND BARBUDA

There has been a great history of advocacy in Antigua and Barbuda over the years stretching back to the days of slavery. Resistance by runaways who settled in what was then Boggy Peak (now Mount Obama) in 1730, the 1736 plot for which National Hero, King Court and other leaders were executed, and the 1831 unrest over the abolition of the Slave Market, are well documented events in the nation's history.

In the intervening, post-Emancipation years, the focus was on the struggle for workers' rights, including Kenny Joe of Betty's Hope estate who, in 1907, was imprisoned for seeking a pay increase for fellow workers; the 1918 urban labour riots led by Sonny Price and George Weston, the latter establishing a local branch of the Pan-Africanist leader, Marcus Garvey's movement in 1924; and the six-month strike of 1950 that remains a flashpoint in the economic and political transformation of Antigua and Barbuda.

Major demonstrations over the years have included the Antigua Trades and Labour Union march on Government in 1948, which called for constitutional reform, and the African Liberation Day march of 1973, led by Leonard 'Tim' Hector and immortalised in King Swallow's winning calypso tune, 'March for Freedom'.

Leonard 'Tim' Hector led the African Liberation Day march of 1973

Where political advocacy is concerned, 1968 was a pivotal year in Antigua and Barbuda. It was the year of a major strike and demonstration that resulted in a state of emergency and a by-election, and ultimately the birth of the nation's two-party system of politics. Today, activist organisations continue to challenge the status quo.

Social transformation, in particular, gender advocacy, plays a significant role. The Directorate of Gender Affairs and a number of advocacy groups raise awareness of contemporary gender issues, from domestic abuse to consent, street harassment to income inequality. The directorate began life in 1980 as the Women's Desk. Today, many groups and individuals activate awareness programmes and practical initiatives tackling everything from empowerment to environment, health to social relief, road safety to the rights of the child, animal welfare to the well-being of humans, and literacy to prison rehabilitation.

Joanne C. Hillhouse

VISITATE QUESTO ANGOLO DI PARADISO: L'INVITO È APERTO A TUTTI

Sono centinaia le ragioni che spingono a visitare Antigua e Barbuda e non stiamo parlando solo delle 365 spiagge, anche se rappresentano un ottimo punto di partenza. Immergersi nelle nitide acque azzurre di un mare tropicale, sentire la finissima sabbia scivolare tra le dita o semplicemente rilassarsi all'ombra di un albero di cocco dà indubbiamente la sensazione di trovarsi in paradiso. Sono ovviamente tipici aspetti di una spiaggia caraibica per eccellenza ma, per alcuni, sono motivi validi abbastanza da visitare questo 'Paradiso in Terra'. Ma Antigua e Barbuda non è fatta solo di spiagge e ha molto più da offrire. Esploriamo tutte le attrazioni... con ben altri dieci motivi.

1 Carnevale: Lo sfarzo e la pompa, la musica calypso e la creatività del Carnevale iniziano tutti gli anni a fine luglio e continuano fino all'inizio di agosto: una festa vibrante e vivace che celebra la cultura, la storia e l'arte di Antigua e Barbuda. Dal basso pulsante della musica agli scintillanti colori delle sfilate, chi può resistere alle travolgenti parate, ai suoni e ai ritmi di questo spettacolare evento?

2 Madre Natura: Con il suo caldo sole tropicale, rilassanti alisei, acque cristalline e una lussureggiante vegetazione, Antigua e Barbuda è un vero e proprio angolo di paradiso. Qui, potrete nuotare con le pastinache, ammirare le tartarughe embricate o farvi sorprendere da una balena che salta fuori dall'acqua; sulla terraferma, invece, non perdetevi un'escursione tra i Monti Shekerley e il Mont Obama oppure tra la Diga di Wallings e la Signal Hill. Ma non solo...avete anche la possibilità di esplorare le isole circostanti, che includono Great Bird Island, sede del serpente corridore, uno dei più rari e pericolosi al mondo.

3 Vela: Antigua e Barbuda ospita svariati eventi di vela, che attirano partecipanti di ogni parte del globo. Uno di questi appuntamenti è l'Antigua Sailing Week, ormai alla sua 48esima edizione e una delle regate più classiche dei Caraibi. Altri eventi velici includono l'Antigua Classic Regatta e il Super Yacht Challenge. Per ospitare queste manifestazioni, Antigua offre porti e servizi marini di classe mondiale, soprattutto presso l'English Harbour.

4 Destinazione cosmopolita: Situata sull'estremità sud-orientale della catena delle Isole Leeward, Antigua e Barbuda si trova nella posizione ideale per fungere da hub per le Isole Windward e il territorio dei Caraibi. Dotato di un nuovo terminale, l'Aeroporto internazionale V.C. Bird è ora il più grande delle Isole Leeward, con un flusso annuo di quasi un milione di passeggeri. Il porto principale del Paese è ubicato nella capitale St John's e permette contemporaneamente l'ormeggio di ben quattro navi da crociera. Per accogliere il loro arrivo, il molo circostante si è trasformato in un affollato centro commerciale dove acquistare prodotti tipici dell'artigianato locale, souvenir e articoli duty free. Un'ampia selezione di alberghi, che racchiude boutique hotel e strutture di lusso, rende Antigua e Barbuda una destinazione attraente per turisti e viaggiatori d'affari di tutto il mondo.

5 Gastronomia: Tra le specialità locali figurano il fungie, il pepperpot, il budino di riso, la patata dolce ducana e il baccalà, lo spezzatino di capra e pane tradizionale cotto a legna. E data la natura cosmopolita del Paese, molti ristoranti, caffetterie e bar servono gustosissime pietanze caraibiche e internazionali... con un tocco decisamente locale.

6 Mango: A dire il vero, non solo il mango, ma una grande varietà di frutti tropicali, che vanno dalla graviola dal gusto dolce alla mela cannella ancora più dolce, dal mamoncillo alla guava, nonché al famoso 'ananas nero' di Antigua. Ma il mango in particolare riveste una posizione di onore in occasione del celebre Mango Fest annuo, che include un concorso per 'bartender' e chef, come se questo frutto estivo non ufficiale nel suo stato naturale non fosse già una delizia per il palato.

7 Storia: Gli edifici e l'architettura coloniale, tra cui le fortificazioni militari, le prigioni per gli schiavi, gli zuccherifici e le chiese, la dicono lunga sulla storia culturale e sociale di Antigua e Barbuda. Il Nelson's Dockyard, ad esempio, prende il nome dall'illustre eroe britannico, l'Ammiraglio Orazio Nelson, stazionato ad Antigua negli anni 1780.

8 Dimensioni: Con un'area di sole 108 miglia quadrate per Antigua e di 62 per Barbuda, la piccola nazione insulare è facile da esplorare sia con un tour organizzato che in auto, taxi, autobus, moto, bicicletta o a piedi. Ad Antigua e Barbuda ci si può muovere liberamente senza rischio di perdersi.

9 Leggende sportive: Già nel solo mondo del cricket, tra i nomi associati ad Antigua figurano Sir Vivian Richards (l'unico ancora vivente a ritenere il titolo di 'eroe nazionale'), Sir Andy Roberts, Sir Curtly Ambrose e Sir Richie Richardson. Gli appassionati dello sport che visitano il Paese, quindi, potrebbero imbattersi in questi e in altre leggende famose, che incarnano la generosa natura degli abitanti di Antigua e Barbuda.

10 Wadadli: È la traslitterazione moderna del nome attribuito ad Antigua dalla popolazione indigena Arawak (il nome dato a Barbuda è Wa'omani). Oggi, il nome viene usato in prodotti vari, in particolare la Wadadli Beer, un ingrediente essenziale per quando ci si concede un po' di 'liming', ovvero il tempo dedicato a rilassarsi e socializzare.

Questi sono solo altri dieci motivi per visitare Antigua e Barbuda e, insieme alle pagine successive, mirano ad estendere a tutti l'invito a venire a godersi una fetta di paradiso.

游览这座迷你天堂的公开邀请函

游览安提瓜和巴布达的原因有很多。一提到这里，人们首先会想到的是此处所拥有的 365
个海滩，但这里的美景不止于此。浸入清澈的蓝绿色热带海水之中，感受脚趾间细腻的滑沙，或者只是在可可树下放松身心，定会有置身天堂之感。这些都是加勒比海滩的部分精华所在，游览这座"人间天堂"的充分理由。但安提瓜和巴布达所拥有的可不仅仅只有这些，您只需走近细细观赏……请参考以下十个理由。

理由一 - 狂欢节：这是每年 7 月末、8
月初举行的盛事，是庆祝安提瓜和巴布达文化、历史和艺术的重大活动。从贝斯音乐弹唱到七彩斑斓令人目眩的群众游行，很少有人能够抵抗得住这种令人心醉神迷的视觉、听觉盛宴，不由自主地跟着动人的旋律翩翩起舞。

理由二 -
大自然母亲：安提瓜和巴布达富有温暖的热带阳光、和煦的信风、清澈的海水、茂盛的植被，堪称人间小天堂。在这里，你可以与黄貂鱼共舞、观赏玳瑁海龟或者亲眼目睹跃出水面的鲸鱼；也可以从谢克力山前往奥巴马山远足，或者从沃岭大坝徒步到信号山；抑或探索岸边诸岛，包括大鸟岛等等，大鸟岛是世界上最稀有且最无害的蛇 - 安提瓜黑绳蛇 - 的家园。

理由三 -
航海：安提瓜和巴布达主办多种航海活动，吸引了来自全球各地的爱好者前来参与。安提瓜航海周就是其中一例，它是加勒比海地区最古老的帆船比赛，现已举办 48
年。其他活动还包括安提瓜经典帆船赛以及超级游艇挑战赛等。为承办这些活动，安提瓜提供有世界级船坞和海洋服务，英吉利港的设施更是举世闻名。

理由四 -
国际化都市：安提瓜和巴布达位于背风群岛链的东南端，它也是向风群岛以及大加勒比地区的交通枢纽。安提瓜和巴布达的新航站楼，维尔伯德国际机场如今是背风群岛最大的机场，每年运送乘客近百万名。该国的主要港口位于首都圣约翰，一次可容纳四艘大型游轮。为庆祝"游轮日"，周边的码头现已成为热门购物中心，主要销售当地的手工艺品、礼品以及免税商品。包括从小型精品酒店到奢华酒店在内的一系列精品酒店，使得安提瓜和巴布达成为来自全球各地的游客及商务人士的首选目的地。

理由五 - 美食：当地特色粥 (fungee)、胡椒羹、米饭布丁、甜薯、咸鱼、山羊水 (goat water)
以及传统木烤面包都是当地备受欢迎的美食。由于安提瓜和巴布达的国际化特质，许多酒店、咖啡馆和酒吧都提供来自加勒比以及世界各地的美食......极具地方特色。

理由六 - 芒果：实际上，从甜番荔枝到甜度更高的释迦果，从及牙买加绿皮葡萄 (guinep)
到番石榴，这里的热带水果不胜枚举。另外，安提瓜特产黑凤梨举世闻名。但是，这里的非正式夏季水果 —
芒果，尤其是在人气极旺的年度芒果节所展示的那些用于"调酒"和大厨比拼的芒果，在自然状态下不适合食用。

理由七 -
历史：这里殖民时期的各种建筑，包括军事堡垒、奴隶地牢、糖厂和教堂等，都是安提瓜和巴布达文化和社会历史的见证。这里有以英国航海英雄霍雷肖·纳尔逊上将命名的纳尔逊船坞，纳尔逊上将于 18 世纪 80 年代曾在安提瓜岛驻扎。

理由八 - 面积:安提瓜岛占地仅 108 平方英里，巴布达岛则为 62
平方英里，无论是跟团还是租车、乘坐公交、搭乘出租车、摩托车、骑自行车或者步行，这两座孪生小岛都非常适合旅游观光。你可以在安提瓜和巴布达到处闲逛而永远也不会迷路。

理由九 -
体育界传奇：仅在板球运动历史上，安提瓜就曾经涌现出维维安·理查兹爵士（安提瓜和巴布达唯一在世的国家英雄）、安迪·罗伯特爵士、科特雷·安布罗斯爵士以及里奇·理查森爵士。对于板球球迷来说，在这里可以见证这些伟人以及其他在板球场上成名的英雄人物的事迹，他们都是志存高远的安提瓜和巴布达人的榜样。

理由十 -
Wadadli：这是当地土著居民阿拉瓦克人称呼安提瓜的名字的现代翻译版（巴布达的名字则是
Wa'omani）。如今，这一名字已成为很多物品的品牌，最知名的当属 Wadadli 啤酒，这是当地人外出闲逛时必备的一种重要食品。

这些只是游览安提瓜和巴布达众多理由中的十条，本文内容以及后面页面中的内容将用作邀请您前来这座人间小天堂游览的公开邀请函。

رابعًا. العاصمة: تيغوا وبربودا تقع في الطرف الجنوبي الشرقي من سلسلةلأن أن جزر ليوارد، فإنها في وضع جيد يؤهلها أيضا للعب دور مركز لجزر ويندوارد وكذلك منطقة البحر الكاريبي على النطاق الأوسع. وفي وجود صالة الركاب الجديدة، أصبح في.سي. يتعامل مع ما يقرب من مطار بيرد الدولي الآن أكبر مطار في جزر ليوارد، و مليون مسافر سنويا. ،يوجد الميناء الرئيسي في البلاد في العاصمة، سانت جون ويمكن أن يستوعب أربع سفن سياحية في وقت واحد. واستجابة لموسم" السفن السياحية" أصبح الرصيف المحيط مركزا شهيرا لتسوق منتجات الحرف اليدوية ، وبضائع السوق الحرة المحلية والهدايا التذكارية. تشكيلة واسعة من الفنادق، من المحلات الصغيرة إلى المتاجر الأفخم، وهذا ما يجعل أنتيغوا وبربودا وجهة جذابة للسياح ورجال الأعمال من مختلف أنحاء العالم.

خامسًا. الطعام: الفونغي، وبيبريبوت، والأرز باللبن، والدوكانا والسمك المملح وغوت خبز القديم والتقليدي في فرن الخشب هي الأطباق المفضلة محليًاووتر، وال. وبفضل الطبيعة العالمية للبلاد، فإن العديد من المطاعم والمقاهي والحانات تقدم بعضًا من أشهى المأكولات في جميع أنحاء منطقة البحر الكاريبي وفي جميع أنحاء العالم... مع لمسة محلية مميزة.

سادسًا. نجوالما: هناك في الواقع الكثير من الفاكهة الاستوائية، بداية من القشطة الشائكة إلى التفاح السكري الأكثر حلاوة، ومن الليمون الإسباني إلى الجوافة وأناناس أنتيغوا الأسود المميز. ولكن المانجو، على وجه الخصوص، تُعرض خلال مهرجان المانجو السنوي الشعبي الذي يضم"الخلط فنانيي" ومنافسة الطاهي، وكأن هذه الفاكهة الصيفية غير الرسمية في حالتها الطبيعية ليست بالفعل وليمة لذيذة.

سابعًا. التاريخ: تتحدث المباني في العصر الاستعماري والهندسة المعمارية، بما في ذلك التحصينات العسكرية، وزنزانات العبيد، ومصانع السكر والكنائس، عن يخ الثقافي والاجتماعي في أنتيغوا وبربوداالتار. ترسانة نيلسون، على سبيل المثال، سميت باسم بطل البحرية البريطانية الأدميرال هوراشيو نيلسون، الذي كان متمركزًا في أنتيغوا في ثمانينات القرن الثامن عشر(1780).

ثامنًا. المساحة: ميلًا مربعًا 62 نتيغوا، وميلًا مربعًا لأ 108 لأن المساحة تبلغ فقط لبربودا، فإن الدورة المكونة من جزيرتين تتميز بالتنقل السهل والأمن. سواء من خلال جولة منظمة أو استئجار سيارة أو حافلة أو سيارة أجرة، دراجة نارية، دراجة هوائية أو سيرًا على الأقدام. فيه بحرية إن أنتيغوا وبربودا هو المكان الذي يمكنك أن تتجول ولكن لن تتوه أبدا.

تاسعًا. الأساطير الرياضية: في لعبة الكريكيت وحدها، أصبحت أنتيغوا موطنًا للسير فيفيان ريتشاردز(البطل القوي الوحيد الذي ظل على قيد الحياة) السير ، اندي روبرتس، السير كيرتلي أمبروز والسير ريتشي ريتشاردسون. بالنسبة لكريكيت، قد يعني الوقت هنا رؤية هذه الألعاب والروائع الأخرىإلى عشاق لعبة ا التي ذاع صيتها في الملاعب والتي تقدم نموذجًا للإرادة القوية لسكان أنتيغوا وبربودا.

عاشرًا. وادادلي: هذه هي الترجمة الحرفية الحديثة للاسم الذي يطلق على أنتيغوا من قبل الشعوب الأصلية الأراواكيم(بربودا هو واومانياس). واليوم يصف هذا الاسم أشياء كثيرة، وأبرزها، بيرة وادادلي، وهي مكون أساسي عند"النقع" (العصر).

هذه ليست سوى عشرة أسباب أخرى لزيارة أنتيغوا وبربودا ولكنها تمثل، مع الصفحات التالية، دعوة مفتوحة لزيارة هذه القطعة من الجنة وتجربتها بنفسك.

وان سيج. هيلهاوس

الـدعوة مفتوحـة لزيـارة قطعـة مـن الجنـة

365هنــاك منـــات الأسبـاب الـتي تـدعوك لزيـارة أنتيغـوا وبـربودا، ليـس فقط لأجـل شـاطئ، علـى الـرغم مـن أن هـذا مـن شـأنه أن يكـون مكانًـا جيـدًا للبدايـة. لا شـيء يعـادل الشـعور بـالعيش فــي الجنــة أكــثر مـن الانغمـاس فـي الميـاه الصـافية والزبرجديـة للبحـر ور بالرمــال الناعمــة بيـن أصـابع قـدميك أو مجـرد الاسـترخاء فـي ظـل الاسـتوائي أو الشـع شـجرة جـوز الهنـد. هـذه هـي بعـض العناصـر الرئيسية لمنظـر شـاطئ البحـر الكـاريبي المـذهل، وربمـا يقـول البعـض، أن هـذه أسبـاب كافيـة لزيـارة"الجنـة علـى الأرض". ،رغـم ذلـك عليـك فقـط إلقـاء نظـرة فاحصـة فـإن أنتيغـوا وبـربودا لـديها الكـثير لتقدمـه، يتعيـن والتفكيـر فـي عشـرة أسبـاب أخـرى ...

أولا- الكرنفـال: يقـام المهرجـان الفخـم والوطنـي والموسـيقي والمبـدع، فـي كرنفـال فـي أواخـر شـهر يوليـو إلـى أوائـل شـهر أغسـطس وهـو احتفـال نـابض بالحيويـة فـي أنتيغـوا نـاكوبـربودا ليتعـرف النـاس علـى الثقافـة والتـاريخ والفـن ه. ومـن النغمـات الجديـدة للموسـيقى إلـى الألـوان المبهـرة فـي مسـيرات مـاس، قليـل هـم مـن يستطيعون مقاومة المشـاهد الحالمـة، والأصـوات والإيقـاعـات فـي هـذه المناسبـة الرائعـة.

ثانيــا- الطبيعـة الأم: ، لأن أنتيغـوا وبـربودا تنعـم بالـدفء والمنـاخ الاسـتوائي والميـاه الصـافية والنباتـات المورقـة، فإنهـا بحـق قطعـة مـن ،والريـاح التجاريـة الهادئـة الجنـة. هنـا، يمكنـك السبـاحة مـع سمـك الـراي، العثـور علـى السـلاحف البحريـة أو مشـاهدة حـوت يخـترق أمـواج البحـر؛ أو، علـى الأرض، صعـود تـلال شـيكرلي إلـى جبـل أوبامـا، أو بمـا فـي ذلـك جزيـرة ،سـد والينغـز إلـى تـل سـنجنال؛ أو استكشـاف الجـزر البحريـة الطيـور العظمـى، الـتي تضـم أنـدر ثعبـان فـي العـالم والأقـل إيذاءً- متسـابق أنتيغـوا.

ثالثــا- الإبحـار: تستضيـف أنتيغـوا وبـربودا عـددا مـن سبـاقات الـزوارق الشـراعية الـتي تجـذب المشـاركين مـن مختلـف أنحـاء العـالم. وفـي هـذه المناسبـات، يشـهد أسبـوع وهـو أقـدم سبـاق للقـوارب فـي منطقـة البحـر 48 ا الآن عامـه الـإبحـار فـي أنتيغـو الكـاريبي. وتشـمل المناسبـات الأخـرى سبـاق القـوارب أنتيغـوا كلاسـيك وتحـدي اليخـوت السـوبر. لاستيعـاب هـذه المناسبـات، تقـدم أنتيغـوا مراسـي السـفن والخـدمات البحريـة، وخاصـة فـي الميـناء الإنجلـيزي.